LISTENING TO BACH

LISTENING TO BACH
The Mass in B Minor *and the* Christmas Oratorio

Daniel R. Melamed

OXFORD
UNIVERSITY PRESS

Oxford University Press is a department of the University of Oxford. It furthers the University's objective of excellence in research, scholarship, and education by publishing worldwide. Oxford is a registered trade mark of Oxford University Press in the UK and certain other countries.

Published in the United States of America by Oxford University Press
198 Madison Avenue, New York, NY 10016, United States of America.

© Oxford University Press 2018

First issued as an Oxford University Press paperback, 2020

All rights reserved. No part of this publication may be reproduced, stored in a retrieval system, or transmitted, in any form or by any means, without the prior permission in writing of Oxford University Press, or as expressly permitted by law, by license, or under terms agreed with the appropriate reproduction rights organization. Inquiries concerning reproduction outside the scope of the above should be sent to the Rights Department, Oxford University Press, at the address above.

You must not circulate this work in any other form and you must impose this same condition on any acquirer.

Library of Congress Cataloging-in-Publication Data
Names: Melamed, Daniel R., author.
Title: Listening to Bach : the Mass in B minor and the Christmas oratorio / Daniel R. Melamed.
Description: New York, NY : Oxford University Press, [2018] | Includes index.
Identifiers: LCCN 2017046684 | ISBN 978-0-19-088105-4 (hardcover : alk. paper) | ISBN 978-0-19-009725-7 (paperback : alk. paper) | ISBN 978-0-19-088107-8 (epub)
Subjects: LCSH: Bach, Johann Sebastian, 1685–1750. Masses, BWV 232, B minor. | Bach, Johann Sebastian, 1685–1750. Weihnachts-Oratorium. | Vocal music—18th century—History and criticism.
Classification: LCC ML410.B13 M34 2018 | DDC 782.32/32—dc23
LC record available at https://lccn.loc.gov/2017046684

For SDRM

Contents

List of Tables		ix
About the Companion Website		xi
Preface		xv
Part I. The *Mass in B Minor* BWV 232		1
	Chapter 1. Performing the *Mass in B Minor* in an Age of Choices	3
	Chapter 2. Listening to Parody in the *Mass in B Minor*	21
	Chapter 3. The Musical Topic of the *Mass in B Minor*	40
Part II. The *Christmas Oratorio* BWV 248		63
	Chapter 4. Parody and Its Consequences in the *Christmas Oratorio*	65
	Chapter 5. Listening to the *Christmas Oratorio* with a Calendar	88
	Chapter 6. The *Christmas Oratorio* in the Shadow of Bach's Passions	108
Epilogue: How to Listen to Bach		125
Appendix: Table		127
Suggestions for Further Reading and Listening		135
Index		143

Tables

Table 1.1. The sections of J. S. Bach's autograph score of the *Mass in B Minor* — 127

Table 2.1. Reuse and parody in the *Mass in B Minor* — 128

Table 3.1. Movements of the *Mass in B Minor* sorted by style — 129

Table 4.1. Parody in the *Christmas Oratorio* — 130

Table 4.2. The use of opening and closing model movements in the *Christmas Oratorio* — 131

Table 5.1. Bach's church cantatas performed in Leipzig in the Christmas season — 132

Table 5.2. The *Christmas Oratorio* at St. Thomas and St. Nicholas Churches in 1734–35 — 133

Table 5.3. Christmas season liturgical calendars, 1734–1750 — 133

Table 5.4. Gospel text in the parts of the *Christmas Oratorio* — 134

About the Companion Website

www.oup.com/us/listeningtobach

Username: Music2

Password: Book4416

Oxford has created a website to accompany *Listening to Bach*. Material that cannot be made available in a book, namely short audio examples, are provided here. Readers are encouraged to consult this resource. These website materials are signaled throughout the text with Oxford's symbol 🎵.

Audio Examples

Most excerpts from the *Mass in B Minor* and the *Christmas Oratorio* are from excellent recent recordings, modeled after Bach's own performances, by the Dunedin Consort directed by John Butt (Linn CKD 354 and CKD 399). They are used with the kind permission of Linn Records, www.linnrecords.com.

Audio Example 1.1. *Mass in B Minor*, "Et in unum Dominum" and following movement(s)

Audio Example 1.2. *Mass in B Minor*, "Confiteor."

Audio Example 1.3. *Mass in B Minor*, "Kyrie eleison I."

Audio Example 2.1. Laments

Audio Example 2.2. Love duets

Audio Example 2.3. *Mass in B Minor*, "Osanna in excelsis," vocal opening and closing instrumental ritornello

Audio Example 2.4. Ritornellos removed

Audio Example 2.5. Opening ritornellos removed

Audio Example 2.6. *Mass in B Minor*, transitions

Audio Example 2.7. *Mass in B Minor*, "Et resurrexit" ritornellos

Audio Example 2.8. *Mass in B Minor*, more transitions

Audio Example 2.9. Metrical regularity

Audio Example 2.10. Reworkings

Audio Example 2.11. *Sanctus* BWV 238

Audio Example 2.12. *Mass in B Minor*, "Gloria in excelsis Deo."

Audio Example 2.13. *Mass in B Minor*, "Et resurrexit," setting of "et iterum venturus est."

Audio Example 2.14. "Lust der Völker, Lust der Deinen" BWV 213/13

Audio Example 2.15. Moments of return

Audio Example 3.1. Georg Philipp Telemann, *Concerto for 2 Horns* TWV 52:D2, third movement

Audio Example 3.2. *Mass in B Minor*, "Confiteor."

Audio Example 3.3. *Mass in B Minor*, two settings of "et expecto resurrectionem mortuorum."

Audio Example 3.4. *Mass in B Minor*, "Credo in unum Deum."

Audio Example 3.5. Giovanni Pierluigi da Palestrina, *Missa sine nomine*, arr. J. S. Bach

Audio Example 3.6. *Mass in B Minor*, "Kyrie eleison II."

Audio Example 3.7. *Mass in B Minor*, "Laudamus te."

Audio Example 3.8. *Mass in B Minor*, opening ritornellos

Audio Example 3.9. *Mass in B Minor*, "Gloria in excelsis Deo."

Audio Example 3.10. *Mass in B Minor*, ritornello movements with no opening ritornello

Audio Example 3.11. *Mass in B Minor*, "passus et sepultus est," immediately followed by "Et resurrexit."

Audio Example 3.12. "Credo in unum Deum" BWV 1080 for a Mass by Giovanni Battista Bassani

Audio Example 3.13. *Mass in B Minor*, "Credo in unum Deum."

Audio Example 3.14. *Mass in B Minor*, "Gratias agimus tibi."

Audio Example 3.15. *Mass in B Minor*, closing ritornellos of imitative movements

Audio Example 3.16. *Mass in B Minor*, "Kyrie eleison I."

Audio Example 3.17. *Mass in B Minor*, "Patrem omnipotentem."

Audio Example 3.18. *Mass in B Minor*, three movements with simultaneous choral declamation

Audio Example 3.19. *Mass in B Minor*, "Dona nobis pacem."

Audio Example 4.1. *Christmas Oratorio*, "Herr, wenn die stolzen Feinde schnauben," vocal material after imitative entrances

Audio Example 4.2. *Christmas Oratorio*, "Nur ein Wink von seinen Händen," vocal opening

Audio Example 4.3. Parodies

Audio Example 4.4. *Christmas Oratorio*, simultaneous choral declamation

Audio Example 4.5. Sleep pieces

Audio Example 4.6. Echo arias

Audio Example 4.7. Trumpet arias

Audio Example 4.8. Arias

Audio Example 4.9. Love duets

Audio Example 4.10. Rage

Audio Example 5.1. Cantatas for Christmas Day

Audio Example 5.2.	Cantatas for the second day of Christmas
Audio Example 5.3.	Cantatas for the third day of Christmas
Audio Example 5.4.	Cantatas for New Year's Day
Audio Example 5.5.	Cantatas for Epiphany
Audio Example 5.6.	Cantata for the Sunday after New Year's
Audio Example 5.7.	Cantatas for the Sunday after Christmas
Audio Example 5.8.	Pastoral sinfonias
Audio Example 5.9.	*Christmas Oratorio*, ending movements of part III
Audio Example 6.1.	"Gaudete omnes populi," arr. Wilhelm Friedemann Bach, from J. S. Bach, "Ein feste Burg ist unser Gott" BWV 80/1
Audio Example 6.2.	*Christmas Oratorio*, "Wie soll ich dich empfangen?"
Audio Example 6.3.	*St. Matthew Passion*, "O Haupt voll Blut und Wunden."
Audio Example 6.4.	*Christmas Oratorio*, "Nun seid ihr wohl gerochen."
Audio Example 6.5.	A dubiously claimed parody
Audio Example 6.6.	A likely parody
Audio Example 6.7.	Felix Mendelssohn, *Christus*, opening movement
Audio Example 6.8.	Gospel ensembles
Audio Example 6.9.	*Christmas Oratorio*, "Ehre sei Gott in der Höhe."

Preface

In 1760, a Leipzig professor of poetry, logic, and metaphysics named Johann Christoph Gottsched, whose words Johann Sebastian Bach had set to music on at least one occasion, published a dictionary of the fine arts. One entry includes this little poem attributed to "Menantes," the pen name of Christian Friedrich Hunold, whose poetry Bach also set:

> Ich liebe sonst kein Thier auf Erden,
> Allein die Katzen nehm ich aus;
> Wo diese wohl geheget werden,
> Da kommt kein Mäuschen in das Haus.
> Ein Wirth ist glücklich in der That,
> Der eine Gute Katze hat.
>
> *I love no animal here on earth,*
> *Excepting cats;*
> *Where one of these is kept,*
> *No little mouse comes into the home.*
> *A householder is fortunate indeed,*
> *Who has a good cat.*

It is difficult to see how this verse is worthy of Gottsched, Hunold, or a learned reference work. The explanation is that it appears in the short article on *parody*, a term Gottsched defines this way: "In poetry, an imitation of another poem, particularly of the lyrical type." Parody was understood, in literary terms, as the creation of one poem based on another, and in fact, this cat poem is the second of two by Hunold that Gottsched provides.

Es sieht doch kein Geschöpf auf Erden	Ich liebe sonst kein Thier auf Erden,
So schön als wie die Weiber aus:	Allein die Katzen nehm ich aus;
Durch die kann man vergnüget werden,	Wo diese wohl geheget werden,
Durch die kommt Segen in das Haus.	Da kommt kein Mäuschen in das Haus.
Der Mann ist glücklich in der That,	Ein Wirth ist glücklich in der That,
Der Gott damit versorget hat.	Der eine Gute Katze hat.
There is no creature on earth	*I like no animal here on earth,*
As beautiful as women;	*Excepting cats;*
Through them one can find delight;	*Where one of these is kept,*
Through them, blessing comes into the home.	*No little mouse comes into the home.*
A man is fortunate indeed,	*A host is fortunate indeed,*
Whom God has provided with one.	*Who has a good cat.*

The cat poem is the derived one; it follows the verse structure, meter, and rhyme scheme of the first, ostensibly more high-minded stanza and, in fact, uses the same six line-ending words along with several other shared phrases and a couple of cleverly transformed grammatical constructions.

At least in theory, Hunold created the second poem by rewriting the first; parody serves here as a so-called mode of invention, a mechanism by which a new work of art can be generated or inspired. *Invention* was understood in the early eighteenth century to be the first stage of the creation of a work of rhetoric or (by metaphor) a poem or piece of music. It is telling that basing a new work on an old one was regarded as invention; this is a reminder that modern ideas of originality do not apply well to the eighteenth century. One could invent based on the inspiration of something that already existed without the pejorative sense of a derivative work.

Now there is no way a reader could know from reading just the second poem that the first lay behind it; it's about a cat, with no evident connection to anything else. But when we set it next to the first poem about a woman, we can see the mechanism by which it was derived and perhaps imagine that we understand its genesis. We might also be inclined to evaluate the new poem in light of the old; perhaps it gains in seriousness because of its association with the apparently more high-minded model, or maybe it looks even more trifling in comparison.

And what should we make of the first poem? Taken on its own, we might find it characteristic of attitudes of the eighteenth century, simultaneously respectful and condescending toward women, and typical in its focus on domesticity. (It's a good reminder of how quickly a text can age, even the text of a musical work whose notes still speak to us.) But the existence of the parody—the derived poem—might make us think again, because there could be a troubling lesson in the ease with which the first poem about a woman is transformed into a new one about a man possessing an animal. The potential meaning comes from the relationship between the two texts. Of course, there is a fundamental question of whether the existence of the later poem says anything at all about the meaning or significance of the original.

This was parody in its literary sense in the eighteenth century. In colloquial modern English, parody is used more loosely, meaning an imitation of something serious that makes fun of it, but there is at least one category of parodies that is surprisingly close to the eighteenth-century understanding: musical ones. Whether they are retexted songs by Weird Al Yankovic (such as "Eat It," a parody of Michael Jackson's "Beat It," or "Pretty Fly [for a Rabbi]," based on "Pretty Fly [For a White Guy]" by The Offspring) or the reworkings of Broadway and movie musicals by *Mad* magazine (such as *Antenna on the Roof*, which puts *Fiddler on the Roof* in a suburban setting), the process is the same: somebody writes a new text matching the old one so that it fits the music. But there is a difference, too, in the assumption that the listener or reader knows both, and that is largely why a parody is funny.

Hunold's cat poem is interesting partly because it shares this feature. Because of its place in a reference work on poetic technique, it is clearly a special case in which a reader sees both the model and the parody. But if Hunold had turned to parody to produce the cat poem simply because he needed a quick bit of verse and had not revealed its origin in an extant work, the reader would presumably never know. This means that all the things we think we understand about the new version and its genesis are exceptional; they are almost never part of the significance of parody. This should make us wonder whether we really do know much about the cat poem just because we happen to know where it came from. Focusing on its origin and derivation would also seem to be an invitation to ignore what the new poem says in favor of focusing on how it came to be.

Why am I writing about a cat poem at the start of a book on Bach's *Mass in B Minor* and *Christmas Oratorio*? The poem and the dictionary article are relevant to Bach's music because the creation of a new text based on an existing one was part of an important phenomenon in early-eighteenth-century music: the use of already-composed music to set new words. The mechanism by which a new work was created (often for a new context and purpose) was poetic parody, at least when both the old and the new pieces carried poetic texts. The word parody has also come to be used for another large category of adaptations: those in which extant music is adapted to fit words that already exist, such as a standard liturgical text. The result is the same—music refitted with a new text—but the process is slightly different.

It is almost impossible, though, to identify a parody by J. S. Bach or George Frideric Handel or any other eighteenth-century composer in which there was any reasonable expectation that a listener would know the model. Musical parody was not intended to shed light on an old work or to make fun of it but rather was a spur to the creative process or a way to reuse a composition. It was an especially valuable technique when a composer had written a piece for a particular occasion and did not expect to be able to use it again for its original purpose. In some sense, it kept good music from going to waste.

Each of the two works by Bach at the center of this book, the *Mass in B Minor* and the *Christmas Oratorio*, was the product of parody, and my sense is that the general literature on these works—program notes, liner notes, and so on—has been dominated by discussions of their parody origin. That, in turn, is probably a reflection of the very high proportion of scholarly and technical writing about them that is devoted to parody. The parody origin of these works and Bach's compositional process in creating them have been irresistible to analysts and historians, and the tendency of experts to pursue these topics has also affected more general writings.

But this is a very limited view and one that is largely cut off from the experience of hearing these works either in the eighteenth century or today. Far more people today recognize the music behind Bach's parodies than could ever have in his own time. Only Bach and perhaps a few of his performers would have known the models for these pieces or even that they were the products of parody at all. The origins of the works are fascinating, but as with Hunold's cat poem, we risk missing a lot if we focus on the compositions' genesis rather than on their musical substance and style. (And it turns out we might also be making some fundamental errors of interpretation by focusing on how they came to be.)

In my earlier book *Hearing Bach's Passions* I wrote about problems we face in confronting old music, including the identity of a work known in multiple versions, the consequences of Bach's staffing of his performing ensemble compared with typical performances today, the attribution of a disputed work, and the problem of lost compositions and attempts at their reconstruction. Overall I asked the question "What are we hearing today?" with an emphasis on the conceptual gulf between the eighteenth century and our time. Those problems still interest me, but so do the issues we face in listening to Bach's music—things that stem directly from Bach's compositional choices and from the experience of the music in performance.

So this book is called *Listening to Bach*, with an emphasis on listening rather than hearing. Most of its chapters are about the musical substance of the works and the experience of listening to them. Parody comes in because it has been the subject of so much writing about the *Mass in B Minor* and the *Christmas Oratorio*; it makes a good starting point in sorting out what we listen for in these works and whether the focus on parody necessarily helps. Chapter 2 (on the *Mass*) and chapter 4 (on the *Oratorio*) take up this issue. We can get closer to an eighteenth-century understanding of these pieces if we step away from our fascination with parody, origin, and genesis and listen carefully and in an informed way to the things that happen in these compositions and to what they are telling us.

Also directly relevant to listening to eighteenth-century music is the matter of musical style, with *style* meant in the strict sense of a way of writing. This is the subject of chapter 3, which discusses the two very different musical styles Bach employs in the *Mass in B Minor* and argues that their reconciliation is the musical topic of the piece. This is something you can learn to listen for and something that is directly relevant to the experience of these works in performance.

The experience of listening to the *Christmas Oratorio* is taken up in a different way in chapter 5, which examines the work's relationship to time and the calendar. Our typical encounter with the work is very different in this respect from that of listeners in Bach's era, and the difference can make us think about how the piece is assembled and what it means to listen to the entire oratorio.

Finally, two chapters deal with the modern reception of the two works, in different ways. Chapter 1 looks at modern performances and recordings of the *Mass in B Minor*, suggesting that every one is ideological and interpretive, whatever approach it takes. Chapter 6 examines aspects of the *Christmas Oratorio*'s reception in the nineteenth and twentieth centuries, a history that has consistently viewed the work primarily in relation to Bach's passion settings, with interpretive consequences for the work and our view of the composer.

With its emphasis on listening, the book all but demands that you read it with access to recordings of the works. An extensive companion website contains many excerpts of the *Mass in B Minor*, the *Christmas Oratorio*, and works by Bach and others for comparison. The section Suggestions for Further Reading and Listening provides ideas on where to start among the many available recordings of each work. Every one of them has something to teach, even more if you learn some new ways to listen to them.

The chapters here draw on up-to-date scholarship on Bach and eighteenth-century music; some material is drawn from my own published research. I have worked out many of the ideas and approaches here in my courses and seminars, and I am grateful to my students for stimulating discussions and insightful research. I am also grateful to colleagues for their assistance, especially Stephen A. Crist, Wendy Gillespie, Robin A. Leaver, Michael Marissen, and Steven Zohn; to Nancy Toff and Alexandra Dauler of Oxford University Press; to Damian Penfold and Wendy Keebler; and to John Butt and Linn Records for the use of extensive excerpts from their excellent recordings of the *Mass* and the *Oratorio*.

And I could not have done any of this without Suzanne.

Bloomington, Indiana
May 11, 2017

LISTENING TO BACH

Part I

THE *MASS IN B MINOR* BWV 232

ONE

Performing the *Mass in B Minor* in an Age of Choices

Is a musical performance ever ideologically neutral?

Buying chocolate used to be pretty simple. There was milk chocolate, dark chocolate for exotic tastes, and unsweetened chocolate for baking. That was about it in the United States, and asking just for *chocolate* probably got you a Hershey-style bar of milk chocolate, maybe with almonds if you specified. But have you tried buying it recently? There is every gradation of cocoa content specified as a percentage, limitless additions and flavorings, organic chocolate, single-origin chocolate, and so on. As a result, you can't just ask for chocolate anymore; there are choices to be made. And if you do opt for a Hershey bar at the checkout counter, you probably realize that you are making a choice for milk chocolate of generic origin and without other flavors or additions. A Hershey bar is still chocolate, but it now represents a series of choices. It has characteristics that went unmentioned before; it used to stand for chocolate generically, but now it is something specific—without having changed.

Something similar has happened to musical performance in general and to Bach's *Mass in B Minor* in particular. Bach's vocal-instrumental works were revived in the middle of the nineteenth century in a movement led by large amateur choral societies. As a result, this repertory left the domain of the professional church musicians who presented it in the liturgy and effectively became the property of choral ensembles that performed it in concerts. Those choirs came to share it with big orchestras and professional soloists, not necessarily for any historically informed reason but first according to the practical conditions of their performances and then simply as the way things were done.

Just as string quartets were self-evidently for four string players, the *Mass* became a work for large chorus, orchestra, and soloists.

Performances further tended to stick to a narrow range of musical texts and of realizations of the work. This was largely because of the influence of particular editions but was also because the very existence of choices was not clear; it probably seemed evident what was to be sung and played, and how. But recognizing that there are choices to be made at every turn and understanding the ideas behind them can open our ears to aspects of a work that we might not have considered. At the least, we might want to make ourselves aware of the choices involved, not to judge or to decide that they might be wrong—there really is no such thing in matters of interpretation—but to appreciate that they are, in fact, choices and that they point to particular views of a work. And indeed, every set of choices represents an interpretation of the *Mass in B Minor*. There are no ideologically neutral performances—no plain, uninflected *Mass*. And as with chocolate, everything is a choice.

The choices in performing Bach's *Mass in B Minor* begin with its musical text. Compared with a lot of Bach's music, the decisions are at the level of detail; for the most part, we are not faced with multiple versions as in Bach's Passion settings, where his reuse and revision of the works over the years left a series of different versions incorporating alternative movements, changed instrumentation, and so on. But details matter, particularly in a work of such cultural significance.

The variants and uncertainties in the text of the *Mass* have mixed origins. Bach made some revisions even after he established the basic musical text of the work. The age and poor condition of the autograph score that transmits the work and the many small interventions entered after Bach's lifetime by his son Carl Philipp Emanuel make it difficult to read the notes in a few places. The number of genuine uncertainties is very small, though, and they are not of much consequence beyond a desire to know precisely what Bach wrote. More significant are the ambiguities, particularly in instrumentation, that arise from the fact that we have only a score from Bach, not performing materials (at least not for the *Mass* strictly construed) of the kind that document a realization. We have to supply important details ourselves.

There are also some problems that stem from the origin of most of the music of the *Mass* in older compositions that Bach reworked. These are, to some extent, problems of our own making, because there is no good reason we should turn to the models when we have a perfectly good score of the *Mass* itself. We should arguably ignore the older uses of this music unless we want to study the process by which Bach created the *Mass*. (This issue is taken up in chapter 2.) But scholarship has set us down this path, sometimes with good or at least understandable reasons, and this can lead to difficulties.

To understand all this and to recognize the choices that performers face, we need to understand the history of the *Mass in B Minor*. Bach composed (or, arguably, assembled) the work in his last year, probably sometime in 1749. We can deduce this largely from evidence of his handwriting, which took on particular characteristics, especially because of a tremor he developed that left obvious traces in his penmanship. Even after he had copied, composed, and assembled the work, he evidently had second thoughts about one sequence of movements in the Credo and made a change. The way he notated the revision left the original fully legible, offering the tempting appearance of two versions from which to choose—and even the possibility of mixing them.

At Bach's death, the autograph score passed to his son Carl Philipp Emanuel, who was responsible for the preservation and survival of a great deal of Bach's church music. The younger Bach evidently recognized the significance of the *Mass in B Minor* and included a portion of it in a benefit concert in 1786 at which he performed the Credo (with an instrumental introduction of his own composition), his own *Magnificat* (a work modeled on his father's setting and heard earlier in Leipzig), his renowned "Heilig" for double chorus, one of his symphonies, and the aria "I know that my redeemer liveth" and the Hallelujah Chorus from George Frideric Handel's *Messiah*. In connection with this performance (and perhaps in other engagement with the work), C. P. E. Bach made corrections and revisions that occasionally obscure what his father had written.

That gives us a fascinating late-eighteenth-century perspective of the piece and a window on its reception, but it also represents a hindrance. Time and the presence of acidic ink, particularly in places overwritten by Emanuel, have led to deterioration of the manuscript's paper, rendering a few passages difficult to read and making us uncertain of precisely what J. S. Bach wrote.

Some of the details can be filled in by common snse (as you just did in interpreting that misspelled word) and others by reference to copies of the *Mass* made from Bach's score when it was more readable than it is today. This is one of the reasons scholars have spent so much effort tracing the origins of secondary copies of the work, attempting to identify the ones that are witnesses to the document in a better state of preservation and before revisions were entered. To be honest, though, almost all the questions that arise concern very small matters indeed, few that most listeners would ever notice, so this is not a big problem.

Some aspects of what we might call the prehistory of the *Mass in B Minor* have presented choices, although in some ways they are artificial. When Bach compiled his complete setting of the Ordinary of the Mass in 1749, he drew extensively on material that already existed. Bach's autograph score consists of four numbered units, each provided with a title page in his hand. Two of the four large units already already existed, and he took them over wholesale: a Kyrie-Gloria setting he had composed in 1733 and a Sanctus setting from 1724. For the first, Bach simply incorporated the manuscript score from 1733; for the second, he made a new copy with a few revisions. (See table 1.1 in the appendix.)

For these two units that predate 1749, we also have sets of performing parts. For the Sanctus, they date from 1724 and were almost certainly used for liturgical performances in the principal Leipzig churches, both in that year and subsequently (as suggested by additional parts dating from later in Bach's tenure). The parts for the Kyrie and Gloria are from 1733, the same year as the score, but their context is very different from that of the Sanctus materials. They were not for performance in the course of Bach's Leipzig duties; rather, they were prepared by Bach and members of his family, on particularly fine paper, for presentation to the Dresden court of the Saxon elector. Together with a formal and obsequious cover letter, they formed Bach's application for an appointment that eventually materialized in a position as court composer in 1736.

These two sets of parts, each prepared under Bach's supervision, represent invaluable evidence for the realization of this music, in one case under Bach and in the second as he mapped it out for others. But none of this performing material documents the *Mass in B Minor*. The Sanctus parts are for a one-movement liturgical work Bach used in Leipzig; the Kyrie and Gloria parts were presumably designed for a performance of the first two portions of the Mass Ordinary in Dresden by the musicians of its court chapel. (There is no evidence that they were ever used.) In 1724 and 1733, the years of those parts, there was no such thing as the *Mass in B Minor*; that work came into being only in 1749, when Bach incorporated this music into a complete setting of the Ordinary.

And what he incorporated was the scores, not the performing material. The Sanctus parts evidently remained part of Bach's working tools, presumably stored in a cabinet in the composer's room at the top of the St. Thomas School building and pulled out when he performed this work. The Kyrie and Gloria parts stayed in Dresden, where Bach had presented them and where they remain today. Bach evidently did not draw on the Sanctus parts—he used a score to make the version in the *Mass*—and demonstrably did not refer to the 1733 Kyrie-Gloria parts when he created the *Mass in B Minor*, so these materials do not tell us about the musical text of the *Mass*.

Perhaps even more important, a set of performing parts documents a realization of an eighteenth-century work and is conceptually different from a score. Art music in the European tradition has tended toward increasing specificity by composers in every realm (tempo, dynamics, articulation, instrumentation, and many other details of performance), at least until some twentieth-century figures began consciously rebelling against the prescriptions of a fully determined score. But many aspects of eighteenth-century performance were considered matters of realization, not composition, and were not reflected in scores.

The distinction can be difficult to make when the performer was the composer, but we face it every time we deal with music from the period, including the *Mass in B Minor*. Eighteenth-century scores leave a lot of things unspecified, from the number of performers on a given vocal or instrumental line, to the makeup of the basso continuo group, to the harmonies the keyboard player was expected to realize, and even to the instrumentation of some movements. These were matters for the realization of the work, and a set of parts represents a particular realization specific to a time, place, context, and performers. A different context might yield a different realization, even in the hands of the composer himself.

Many people still refer to the Dresden Kyrie and Gloria as an "early version" of the *Mass in B Minor* (including in the scholarly complete edition of Bach's music and even in its revised volume), but this is a deeply problematic designation. The Dresden parts for the Kyrie and Gloria do not belong to the first part of the *Mass in B Minor*; they are for a 1733 composition that stood on its own. Bach did not compose and assemble that work in 1733 with the idea that it was the early version of anything; it was a piece in its own right. To call it an early form of the *Mass* is teleological, painting Bach's work on this composition as preparation for the *Mass* in 1749. It is understandable that a piece that the nineteenth-century owner of Bach's autograph score called "the greatest artwork of all times and all peoples" would inspire teleological thinking, but we still should not lose sight of how misleading it is to regard the 1733 work as a form of the *Mass in B Minor*.

Nor should we think of its performing parts as documents of the full *Mass*. Those parts (like those of the Sanctus) represent Bach's realization of a portion of this music for performance in a particular context. Given the number of details left unspecified in the score of the *Mass*, we can be grateful for this guide to Bach's realization of the work if we hope to perform it. But, again, the Dresden parts are not a realization of the Kyrie and Gloria of the *Mass in B Minor*. They represent one set of choices for an earlier composition presumably aimed at particular musicians Bach hoped would perform the work in a specific context. There is nothing in these parts that stands outside the range of usual eighteenth-century practice; we just need to remember how specific these documents are. We can also note that there are differences between this realization and Bach's own Leipzig church performing practice. This should not surprise us, given the different context, but is a good reminder that even under Bach, there was no singular way to realize this kind of music.

This matters because some of what we "know" about the *Mass in B Minor* actually represents our understanding of Bach's older realizations of the underlying pieces. That is, performers have tended to realize the Kyrie and Gloria of the *Mass in B Minor* according to the Dresden parts and the Sanctus mostly according to the 1724 parts. We can certainly choose to take cues from those versions, but that is a choice. This point has typically not been reflected in performing editions of the work, which have tended silently to fold evidence from outside the 1749 score into their presentations of the piece. Recent scholarship has devoted a lot of energy to undoing apparent truths and to encouraging a fresh look (and choices).

The most audible choices we have to make lie elsewhere in the *Mass in B Minor*. One particularly striking problem concerns the Credo, in which the composer rethought the number of movements and the distribution of the text. The words "Et incarnatus est" were originally part of the duet "Et in unum Dominum," which was followed by the "Crucifixus." After entering this sequence of movements in the score, Bach changed his mind and extracted the words "Et incarnatus est de Spiritu sancto ex Maria virgine et homo factus est" from the end of the "Et in unum." Compositionally, he did this by redistributing the text of the "Et in unum Dominum," spreading the now-shortened text across the original music so that it ended with the words "descendit de coelis" (audio example 1.1a) 🔊.

The movement's musical substance was left largely unchanged; in fact, only the vocal lines were revised, and this is reflected in the manner in which Bach made the change physically. Instead of recopying the movement, he left it in place and wrote out just the revised vocal lines on a new page. That is, the instrumental lines remained unchanged, and the new vocal lines were written down on their own. The additional page is headed "Duo Voces Articuli /2°" and has been misinterpreted in a telling way. In some otherwise well-informed writings, you will read theological explanations of this heading, usually something connected with the movement's supposed expression of the oneness of the trinity—two voices "articulate" something—but that is not what this means. Bach wrote the number 2 as an ordinal; it means *second*, not *two*. And the Latin grammar is clear; the heading actually reads "Two voices of the second article." This makes perfect sense. There are several ways to divide and number the sections of the Nicene Creed, but in every one, the second unit begins "Et in unum Dominum Jesum Christum." And a section of a creed is called an article, as in the English expression *article of faith*, so Bach's heading thus means "the two voices belonging to the second article," a straightforward and practical label explaining where these new musical lines belonged.

That some commentators would reach first for a theological interpretation is symptomatic of a tendency to look for esoteric religious meaning in every detail of Bach's work. (I wonder whether there might be an attempt in this case to draw a parallel with a genuinely mystical inscription, "Christus Coronabit Crucigeros" [Christ will crown the cross bearers], that Bach added to one of his canons known as BWV 1077.) Bach undoubtedly made musical choices in response to theological elements, and scholarship steeped in eighteenth-century Lutheran thought has contributed to understandings along these lines. There may well be theological significance to Bach's reconfiguration of this part of the Credo, but that significance seems unlikely to lie in an annotation in the autograph score. We value Bach as a composer, but interpreters often seem to assume that he expressed himself in cryptic religious code rather than in notes.

Having removed the words "Et incarnatus est" from the duet, Bach composed a new choral setting of them, writing out the movement on a new page and cueing its insertion at the end of the "Et in unum Dominum." As a final step in the revision, he added a few measures to the beginning of the "Crucifixus." This movement had begun immediately with voices, but Bach added four instrumental measures at the opening, presumably as a buffer between the choral cadence of the "Et incarnatus est" and the start of the "Crucifixus," and to point the listener's ear even more closely toward the four-measure repeating bass that underlies the entire "Crucifixus." (The added measures represent one cycle of that repeating bass, played by instruments alone before the entrance of voices.)

So there are evidently two versions of this part of the Credo. In the first, the "Et incarnatus est" text is part of the "Et in unum Dominum" movement, which leads directly to the "Crucifixus." The other, entered in the autograph score later, ends the "Et in unum Dominum" with the words "descendit de coelis," presents the words "Et incarnatus est" in their own movement, then presents the "Crucifixus" prefaced by a few new measures (audio example 1.1b) 🎧.

It seems clear that we should probably choose one version (all the text in the duet, without the chorus) or the other (shortened text in the duet, with the chorus). But the editor of the most influential modern edition of the *B-Minor Mass*—the one in the scholarly critical edition of Bach's music—made a curious decision on this point by including the words "Et incarnatus est" both in the duet and in the following chorus. The revised duet is presented as a "variant" at the end of the Credo. The editor did this because of his theory—mistaken, it turns out—that the surviving sources of the *Mass* document several stages of revision by Bach himself and that his "final version" went back to the first form of the duet. The editor does not say why he also includes the "Et incarnatus est" movement but I suspect that it was because, well, it's the "Et incarnatus est."

If our present understanding of the layers of this piece is correct, then you have to know (and choose) to use that "variant" version of the duet (the one in the back) if you perform the chorus. As printed, the edition offers an implicit invitation to perform the piece with the first version of the duet together with the chorus, duplicating the "Et incarnatus est" text.

Of the fifty-five (!) recordings of the *Mass in B Minor* available on a streaming service at the time of this writing, forty-five use the shortened text in the duet followed by the chorus—that is, the final layer in Bach's autograph. Ten of the recordings, probably directly or indirectly under the influence of that edition, include the "Et incarnatus est" text both in the duet and in the chorus. (They are, incidentally, a mixture of traditional and performance-practice oriented recordings.) None omits the "Et incarnatus est" chorus, and it seems likely that nobody was able to imagine a version of the *Mass in B Minor* without this movement—certainly not one they planned to sell to customers expecting to hear it. The hybrid version heard in those ten recordings does not correspond to either of Bach's but conflates them, perhaps simultaneously privileging Bach's first (most inspired?) thoughts and incorporating a favorite movement. More likely, these recordings simply followed the authority of a critical edition that appears to endorse this combination.

Indeed, this 1954 edition of the *Mass in B Minor* (edited by Friedrich Smend) and the critical report that followed a few years later carried the authority of the *New Bach Edition* and its aims of scholarly rigor and objectivity. It was one of the first two volumes of the new edition to appear and carried great symbolic significance, not least as confirmation of the reemergence of German musical scholarship less than ten years after the end of World War II. But as scholars noted right from the edition's publication, it is an idiosyncratic volume that mixes critical editing with a strong desire to bolster particular theories about the *Mass in B Minor*.

One of Smend's deeply held beliefs was that the label *Mass in B Minor* was a nineteenth-century invention. He was correct—we have no title page or any other designation from Bach that calls it that—but Smend went further in arguing that it was wrong to think of this collection of movements as a Mass at all. The title page of his edition makes this point clearly, labeling the work in large letters "Missa / Symbolum Nicenum / Sanctus / Osanna, Benedictus, Agnus Dei et Dona nobis pacem" (from Bach's four title pages) and then adding, in very small type, "called: Mass in B minor." Smend's preface and critical commentary argue that the music in the edition represents four independent works, not a complete Mass setting. Smend stresses the Lutheran context of the work, and in fact, his desire to demonstrate that this collection of pieces is not a complete Catholic Mass colors every aspect of his work, including his evaluation of sources.

Smend's decision to print the long text of the duet and the separate "Et incarnatus est" rests partly on his preference for text-illustrative features of the piece that work better, in his view, in the longer version. And that view, in turn, probably reflects his conviction that the movement was an original composition, not a parody. (This does not appear to be the case, as there is evidence that an older movement does lie behind the "Et in unum Dominum" and that neither the long-text nor the short-text version of the duet was originally composed to these words.) But a stronger motivation for Smend was probably connected with his assertion that the Credo, of which these movements are a part, was an independent and free-standing work, just as each of the four units of the *Mass* was in his view. That belief, which was connected to his conviction that the components of the *Mass in B Minor* were fundamentally Lutheran, was bolstered in Smend's view by what he saw as the Credo's symmetrical construction.

His assertion was that Bach organized the Credo's movements in a "chiastic cycle" with a doubly framed center:

| Credo Patrem | Et in unum | Et incarnatus est Crucifixus Et resurrexit | Et in Sp. Sanctum | Confiteor Et expecto |

In Smend's argument, this construction went beyond the musical to represent a theological underlining of fundamental Christian belief in Jesus's human incarnation, crucifixion, and resurrection (the topics of the three movements in the middle)—with, it was claimed, a distinctly Lutheran emphasis on the crucifixion. This view of the work requires the nine-movement form of the Credo and the inclusion of the separate "Et incarnatus est." Combined with Smend's artistic preference for the long-text version of the duet and his assertion that the new sequence of movements made more sense harmonically, this led him to present a mixed version that corresponded to neither of Bach's.

The very claim that the Credo is "symmetrical" is characteristic of twentieth-century Bach interpretation; the concept figures in many analyses of Bach's music, particularly the sacred works. For example, the central narrative portion of the *St. John Passion* BWV 245 is often claimed to be symmetrically articulated by repeated and closely parallel movements; the motet "Jesu, meine Freude" BWV 227 is likewise always described as symmetrical in its construction. It is true that one can make diagrams on paper that display graphical symmetry, but it is rarely clear what musical claim is being made when this concept is invoked or what *symmetry* means for an art that unfolds in time, not space. The meaning of symmetry, when it is not vague and supposedly self-evident, is usually theological; Bach is almost always said to be accomplishing something religiously interpretive by this construction. But once again, commentators often seem more concerned with esoteric matters than with musical ones.

An article published forty years after Smend's edition attempted to defend his result by arguing that Bach intentionally designed two versions of the piece to reflect confessional differences between Lutheran and Catholic practice and that the two versions represent alternatives, not successive thoughts. Its arguments are fully unconvincing on source-critical grounds, but it also seems symptomatic that these interpreters, too, are convinced that there must be subtle theological reasons for Bach's compositional decisions at every level.

Smend's mixed version, reflecting neither of Bach's, has had consequences, resulting in recordings and performances in which the "Et incarnatus est" text is heard twice. Before we reject this as out of the question, we should recall that there is another place in the *Mass in B Minor* where Bach does repeat a segment of text in two very different settings. The luminous end of the "Confiteor" and the beginning of the "Et expecto resurrectionem" both present the words "Et expecto resurrexionem mortuorum," with completely contrasting affective characters. This is a very nice reflection of the two paradoxically conflicting meanings of death in the Christian faith, expressing both by presenting two settings of the same words. And Bach repeats the words "Credo in unum Deum" in the second movement of the *Mass* even as he begins the new text "Patrem omnipotentem." Bach might thus plausibly have repeated the words "Et incarnatus est" with similar intent, but the way he notated his revision suggests strongly that this was not what he had in mind. It would have been simple to have left the duet text as it was and to have inserted the new "Et incarnatus est" chorus, but Bach went to the trouble of composing new vocal lines for the duet as replacements.

So what should a performance do with the "Et incarnatus est" text today? There are many different grounds for choosing: respect for the authority of an edition and its editor, belief in an interpretive theory put forth in an article, a desire to follow Bach's first design, a preference for Bach's considered final thoughts, a search for the "best version" (whatever that might be), a desire to stick to a performing tradition, or an instinct for a version that includes all the favorite movements. I think you can see that any choice, however made, represents an interpretation.

In fact, there are relatively few such problems requiring a choice of movements in the *Mass in B Minor*. Where things get more ambiguous is in questions of how to realize the work in performance. In a few movements, Bach's score does not provide much guidance on who sings and plays, especially in the realm of instrumentation. For example, the five vocal lines of the "Confiteor" appear in the autograph score without labels. Bach's notation makes the voice assignments clear, because the so-called clefs at the start of each musical line (the symbols that show what pitch is indicated by each line or space on the staff) were conventionally different for each kind of voice in Bach's time. So we know that the five lines are for two sopranos, alto, tenor, and bass, but what about instruments? None is indicated in the "Confiteor." Is this really the first movement of the work in which no instruments participate other than basso continuo?

A purely vocal performance might be plausible, because all of the musical substance of this movement is contained in the five vocal lines (and the basso continuo). It is a piece in old-style counterpoint with no independent role for instruments, constructed in emulation of the music of Giovanni Pierluigi da Palestrina and his sixteenth-century contemporaries (a topic discussed in detail in chapter 3). So the piece is musically complete with just voices in the sense that there are no empty measures or gaps in the texture. But we know that in movements like the "Confiteor," Bach typically paired each voice with woodwinds or string instruments or both, doubling the vocal lines. He did this in his performances of music by Palestrina and in cantata movements that borrowed from the old style to set ancient hymn tunes and certain kinds of scriptural texts. For example, he did this in the second "Kyrie" of the *Mass in B Minor*, and in fact, we know of no Bach performance of music of this kind that did not use doubling instruments.

This practice, typical of Bach's time and tied to the musical style of a movement, was often not reflected in scores; there was little point in using up manuscript paper to write out an identical line for an instrument. Instead, instrumental doubling was often left to the realization of works in performance. A director who wanted an oboe to join a soprano line would have that line copied into a part and given to an oboist; the score might never reflect this or might simply indicate broadly that instruments double. We have plenty of examples in Bach's music in which a set of performing parts tells us about his realization of the work beyond the skeletal notation in the score, including the assignment of doubling instruments in this kind of movement.

But we have no performing parts for the *Mass in B Minor*. Even if we want to be guided by Bach's realization of older uses of the music of the *Mass*, we have performing material only for the Kyrie-Gloria and the Sanctus; there is nothing for the Credo, so we are on our own in deciding how to realize the "Confiteor."

Performers who add instruments to this movement base their decision on their reading of the piece, deeming it stylistically appropriate for doubling and consistent with Bach's documented practice. That sounds sensible and agrees with what we know of Bach's performing, but we need to remember that it represents an interpretation. What is more, there are several possible ways to distribute instruments, depending on what assumptions one makes about the size and composition of the work's vocal and instrumental forces in the first place or even on one's taste in orchestration. These are interpretive choices, and one has to make them one way or the other.

This is mostly hypothetical, as it turns out, because in the absence of instructions from the composer and presumably under the influence of Smend's edition (and others), almost nobody follows eighteenth-century practice or Bach's many models for this kind of movement. A survey of those fifty-five recordings turns up only one that adds doubling instruments to the "Confiteor," conducted by Helmuth Rilling--and his other available recording joins all the others in presenting this movement for voices and continuo only. (audio examples 1.2a and 1.2b) ◉. Another recording labels the movement for "chorus a cappella," making explicit the connection with old-style music but ignoring the eighteenth-century performance practice of this kind of movement. It is good to see this (perhaps obvious) recognition of the movement's style, but the performance does not correspond to Bach's practice. It is also striking that many recordings perform the movement in an affective way, adding an expressive element that is at odds with its musical style; this kind of piece was understood as affectively neutral, in contrast to the expressive goals of modern-style pieces.

Once again, the realization of the "Confiteor" without instruments probably owes a lot to influential editions. The one published by the Bach Gesellschaft, the nineteenth-century complete-works predecessor to Smend's edition for the *New Bach Edition*, rejects instrumental participation in the "Confiteor," even though it cites some manuscript copies from the late eighteenth century that specify it. The editor, Julius Rietz, wrote that he had no doubt that Bach's intention was a performance by chorus and continuo only. His justification was that the imposing instrumental opening of the "Et expecto resurrectionem" by the "full orchestra" points to this conclusion; I can only guess that he particularly valued the contrast of the concerted "Et expecto resurrectionem" with a pure a cappella ideal represented by the "Confiteor" performed without doubling instruments.

Choosing to dispense with doubling instruments in the "Confiteor" altogether, which almost every recording does, sounds like a careful, minimally interpretive approach: we should simply do what the score says, adding nothing that isn't by Bach—and Bach says nothing about instruments in the autograph score of this movement. But there are echoes here of a way of performing Bach and much baroque music "as written." This aesthetic arose in the second half of the twentieth century as a reaction against heavily interpreted performances influenced by nineteenth-century expressive ideals. The result, which you will recognize if you listen to certain recordings from the 1950s and 1960s, was a performance style that many would call mechanical, with rock-steady tempos, absolutely even accents, minimal ornamentation, and fixed loud and soft dynamic levels with nothing in between. It took the historical-performance movement of the 1970s and after to infuse this music with expressivity again, freeing performers to do more than what the score appeared to say. (Whether this kind of singing and playing, certainly more interesting to listen to, is really free of modern ideals is a problem in itself; there is strong evidence that it is not.)

But in fact, this strategy of doing what Bach's score says in the "Confiteor" and nothing else, though seemingly respectful, itself draws on a nineteenth-century ideal of old-style counterpoint as pure vocal music unsullied by instrumental participation. The approach has a loose parallel in art history. It's a little like Greek and Roman sculpture, admired since the Renaissance for the supposed purity of its expression in white marble but now known to have been brightly painted in its own era. The whiteness is an accident of time, and the aesthetic of cool chasteness that many have come to love is a product of modern interpretation and peeling paint. A performance of the "Confiteor" without instruments that literally follows Bach's score—in pure white, perhaps?—actually leads to a strongly ideological reading, just as much as one that chooses a particular instrumentation. It connects Bach's vocal music with an imagined ideal of older sacred works—and not just with the old works but with a particular view of them. Choosing not to intervene here, avoiding doubling instruments, is itself an interpretation; there is no escape. (I suppose these performances might arise out of lack of concern for the possibilities. But this is an ideology, too, reflecting a view that modern performances should simply follow the musical notation and what it appears to mean today.)

It is only fair to acknowledge here that the matter isn't entirely settled; there are indications in Bach's autograph score that can reasonably be interpreted as pointing to a purely vocal realization of the "Confiteor." They appear at the start of the next movement, the "Et expecto resurrectionem," where the layout of the page prompted Bach to put rests in all the instruments as the voices and continuo conclude the "Confiteor." This could imply that the instruments have been silent all along and that the "Confiteor" was performed without doubling. My instinct tells me that this is not how a movement like this would typically have been performed in the eighteenth century and that the notation is ambiguous. But the arguments are plausible.

Perhaps the biggest choice facing modern performers of the *Mass in B Minor* concerns musical forces. Today we might catalog the forces needed to perform the *Mass* as consisting of an orchestra, a chorus, and soloists. But to start with, eighteenth-century conceptions of vocal forces were different, and the categories of "chorus member" and "soloist" did not really exist, at least not in the ways we think of them now. Vocal-instrumental works were staffed principally by a core group of singers, one in each vocal range, responsible for all the music—solo and choral—throughout a piece. A realization of a work might also include additional singers who joined those principal singers in choral movements, but the relationship was not "soloists" and "chorus members" but rather principal singers and supporting ones.

Principal singers sang everything (both solo music in their range and the line for their voice type in choruses); supporting singers joined choral movements to double them. Soloists did not sit quietly in front, dressed especially nicely, waiting for their turn to sing; they participated in every choral movement and formed the core of the chorus or its entirety. Choral movements were characterized more by the participation of all the singers, and by musical style, than by the sound of a massed ensemble (audio examples 1.3a and 1.3b) 🔊.

There are many consequences, but one is that performances of works like the *Mass in B Minor* typically used much smaller vocal forces than we are accustomed to today. This is largely because the number of additional singers was usually small, if they were used at all. It should be stressed that we have no performing parts from Bach for the *Mass* and do not know of any performing context for the work, so we cannot say how a performance of it would have been staffed in Bach's time, just how forces were conceived and what was broadly typical.

There is also evidence that eighteenth-century musicians did not think of instrumentalists as clearly belonging to a different category from singers. Church music ensembles consisted of vocalists and players probably regarded as having a more complementary and collaborative relationship than is sometimes imagined today. Instrumentalists were likely not thought of as "accompanying" singers; in fact, the small size of typical vocal ensembles meant that instrumentalists outnumbered singers in many kinds of music and may well have been heard as more essential. The very musical construction of movements in modern styles emphasizes the instruments in many ways.

An eighteenth-century performance of a work like Bach's *Mass in B Minor* would have started with individual voices on each of the vocal lines, possibly adding additional singers for performances in which larger choral forces were typical, desired, or available. There were places and occasions in which a performance would have been recognizably choral along the lines of some (smaller) modern performances, although the massed forces of a modern orchestra and large chorus were not part of early-eighteenth-century practice.

These issues have been much discussed and debated in recent years, and one of the most interesting consequences is that this perspective has changed the meaning of the traditional way of performing the *Mass* with choir, soloists, and orchestra. It has made this kind of performance into a choice—indeed, a choice whose nature has effectively been hidden for much of the work's recent history, because it long seemed self-evident that the *Mass in B Minor* called for singers and instrumentalists deployed this way. (This is the Hershey bar problem—a choice we did not realize we were making.)

We can trace the origins of this situation. The revival of Bach's concerted vocal music took place in the middle of the nineteenth century and was led by amateur choral societies, particularly in Germany. The pioneers were the members of the Berlin Sing-Akademie, particularly under the leadership of its longtime director Carl Friedrich Zelter. Zelter's work with the Sing-Akademie's amateur chorus, most of whose singing was in private rehearsal and study before it began giving public performances, set the stage for the group's public presentation of Bach's *St. Matthew Passion* BWV 244 in 1829 under the direction of Felix Mendelssohn. The group's study and rehearsal of great music of the past was regarded as part of a process of edification and character building among the middle and upper classes; the music was a vehicle for larger cultural aims.

Because this repertory was cultivated by groups with these goals (and for a long time, by nobody else), it effectively became the property of choral ensembles, and performances were organized along lines that fit their mission. Choruses were large to give the broadest possible educational opportunity and to put difficult music within reach of amateur singers through strength in numbers (and also to appeal to new aesthetic ideals of massed choral sound). Instrumental ensembles were proportionally large to match the voices and in keeping with contemporary orchestral practice, and they might be staffed by professionals who supported the amateur choristers. Soloistic lines were entrusted to professional singers, establishing a clear division between them and chorus members that seems obvious to us today but does not correspond to early-eighteenth-century thinking. It is worth stressing that these ensembles were assembled not for any historically informed reason but to match the philosophical goals, institutional structure, and practical needs of the sponsoring organization.

This persisted. Performances of Bach's Passions and of the *Mass in B Minor* were long most likely to be organized by an amateur or collegiate chorus or a church choir, and this usually dictated the disposition of voices and instruments. The approach taken in the mid-nineteenth century also had aesthetic and interpretive consequences. Until the 1950s, performances of the *Mass in B Minor* might vary in some respects, but essentially all were presented with forces like these, typically designed to be moving, devout, and monumental, in keeping with a shared understanding that came from the received tradition.

This is a generalization, of course, but it is documented by the legacy of recordings of the work beginning in the late 1920s, even those in the 1950s that experimented with smaller ensembles (still choral and orchestral with soloists). The *Mass in B Minor* was a major choral-orchestral piece calling for large groups of singers and instrumentalists, and this implied a monumentality that is still valued today. That is made clear by a DVD recording promoted with the words "Live at Notre Dame Cathedral! Vast acoustics/surroundings!" Apparently, it went without saying that vastness was appropriate to the *Mass*, and to one degree or another, this has been considered true from the time the work entered the concert repertory.

There is no longer an unmarked performance of the *Mass in B Minor*. The producers of that Notre Dame recording chose to project the *Mass* foremost as powerful and awe-inspiring, and that represents an interpretation, not some inherent and self-evident truth about the piece. (Or at least, its marketers did; the recording itself does not consistently come across that way.) Fifty years ago, this would simply have been a recording of the *Mass in B Minor*, but things do not look so self-evident now or so uniform. Now we are more likely to recognize it as reflecting choices in the presentation of the work; it is a modern, large-forces performance that emphasizes the work's grandeur.

We have moved beyond the point of universal agreement (reassuring though it might have been) on performances of the *Mass in B Minor* and how they should sound, and there is a range of possibilities open to performers. We know a great deal, for example, about the execution of concerted vocal music in Bach's time and under his direction and can be guided by that information if we wish. Or we can turn to the long tradition of modern-era performances, including those representing various theories about style and the use of forces.

One thing has surely changed in all of this: recordings are almost all professional now, whether they use a minimal number of singers or a small choir or a large one; the amateur choral-society performances that once formed the core of the recorded legacy of the *Mass in B Minor* are now the exception. One has to hope that performances with amateur forces still take place in communities and universities because the opportunity of learning this music from the inside is still worthwhile—maybe not for the reasons of moral edification promoted by early-nineteenth-century Germans, but musically meaningful nonetheless.

Whatever we do, we need to recognize that each performance reflects choices and represents an interpretation; there is no ideologically neutral presentation. We have to choose, and in this respect, perhaps, performances of the *Mass in B Minor* are now a lot more like chocolate.

TWO

Listening to Parody in the *Mass in B Minor*

Is parody overrated?

It is striking that so much writing about the *Mass in B Minor*, both scholarly and in general texts such as program notes, takes up the topic of parody, the origin of most of the *Mass* in music Bach had composed for other texts and other purposes. (See table 2.1 in the appendix.) In music, the term *parody* was occasionally used in the sixteenth century to refer to the technique of basing one piece (say, a Mass setting) on another (for example, a motet). This understanding of the word became commonplace in modern music history for referring to the technique behind a work such as Tomás Luis de Victoria's *Missa O quam gloriosum*, which draws its musical material from the composer's motet "O quam gloriosum." In the eighteenth century, parody was understood as a poetic process, the taking of an extant poem as the basis for the construction of a new one. In this sense, it was a so-called mode of invention, a tool for dealing with the continuous challenge of the blank page. Music history appropriated the term to refer to the kind of adaptation and reuse of old music with new words represented by much of Bach's *Mass in B Minor* and *Christmas Oratorio*.

There are actually two kinds of adaptations of older music that tend to be called parody today that employ somewhat different processes and produce different results. One follows the literary model in using extant music for a newly written poetic text constructed to match the original verse; this is how much of the *Christmas Oratorio* was put together. The second kind involves a fixed text for which the composer seeks an appropriate (extant) musical setting. Bach's Mass Ordinary settings derived from cantata movements (BWV 233–36 and the *Mass in B Minor*) fall into this category, fitting liturgical Latin prose to settings mostly designed for German poetry.

There are lots of reasons one might want to study the parody process. Perhaps the best justified is an interest in how Bach created a musical work and a desire for insight into his working methods. Those become a little less mysterious when we can compare a derived composition with a model and see how Bach created the new setting from it. Another reason is the love of a good puzzle, particularly when the investigation involves a search for evidence that a movement is a parody even though we no longer have a model composition on which it was based. (In the *Mass in B Minor*, that is true for most of the Kyrie and Gloria and for much of the Credo.)

The sport of matching extant Bach movements with texts he is thought to have set (of which there are a good number preserved in commemorative prints and similar sources but without music) has occasionally been taken to speculative extremes. This sort of pursuit is sometimes extended into attempts to reconstruct a lost piece thought to underlie a *Mass* movement. That is a risky process in some ways, a little like trying to unbake a cake into its ingredients, and we can't know what sorts of changes Bach might have made along the way. Still, there are sometimes features in a musical work that suggest an origin in an older setting and the possibility of imagining at least the outlines of a lost composition.

But we have to acknowledge that the study of parody has very little to do with the sound of the new work, its meanings, or the act of listening. Parody isn't audible, at least not when it is done well, and Bach was good at it. A listener does not simultaneously hear a Mass movement and its underlying model composition, and that is true both for the eighteenth century and for listeners today. Only a very few people besides the composer, if any, would have been in a position to recognize reused music. There are probably lots more today who know the model compositions behind Bach's parodies because so many listeners have absorbed so much of Bach's music. But the only reason most modern listeners have any idea in the first place that much of the *Mass in B Minor* originated in parody is that somebody has told them; it is almost certainly not something they discerned from listening to the work. (A few things in a parody might be audible; chapter 4 takes up this subject in relation to the *Christmas Oratorio*.)

So what is a listener supposed to do with the knowledge that Bach's notes originally carried different words? It takes a technical and thorough knowledge of both compositions to process this as one listens, and it is difficult to say how we might listen in this way to the many parody movements for which no model survives.

If the potential benefit does not lie in listening, that leaves interpretation; perhaps an awareness of the parody origins of a movement is supposed to help us understand the derived piece. This turns out to be a very problematic approach, whose difficulties also affect other kinds of musical interpretation.

In the search for critical approaches to works of art such as musical compositions, modern scholarship has come to acknowledge that assertions about a piece's meaning—what meanings it generates for its listeners, what it signifies, how it is understood—are fundamentally about the listeners in their particular time and place and about what they have absorbed from the culture around them. Meaning is not inherent in a work; it is contingent, depending on the listener and the context. This represents a change from the view that a piece embodies some particular meaning and that the role of interpretation is to figure out what that is, in absolute terms.

Nonetheless, the understandable desire to get to the bottom of works of art leads interpreters to try all kinds of strategies, a few of which are now recognized as fundamentally flawed. Perhaps the most famous of the many fallacies of interpretation is the so-called intentional fallacy: the idea that we can understand a work of art by knowing its creator's intent. On the surface, this might seem plausible. If you want to know what a work of art means, ask the artist what he or she had in mind. With living artists, you can probably see problems right away, starting with our inability to interpret reliably what an artist says. An explanation might or might not be genuine or literal, or it might come well after the creation of the work and represent an entirely new view, or it might raise flags that should make us suspicious of the artist's purpose in answering. There is no way to know the state of mind and intentions of a deceased artist, either; we can't evaluate statements about a work's meaning (if there are any) and certainly can't guess how biographical details might have translated into artistic intent. (Not that people don't try.)

There is simply no way to know an artist's intent, and even if we could, we don't experience or hear intent; we hear a piece of music or see a visual artwork or read a book. Pieces mean what they mean as their listeners understand them. A good musical example might be Ludwig van Beethoven's Ninth Symphony, with its vocal setting of Friedrich Schiller's ode "To Joy" in its last movement. That poem had particular meanings in its time and was understood by the composer in specific ways. Today the symphony and its text are associated with all kinds of things—New Year's celebrations (especially in Japan), observance of special moments in the histories of orchestras and choruses, or the fall of the Berlin Wall in 1989 and the resonance of "freedom" now associated with the piece in the wake of that event. One cannot simply claim that the Ninth Symphony does not mean those things today because they are not what the composer intended or that the modern listeners and interpreters are wrong in hearing the piece as they do. Beethoven's symphony means what it means; there is no use in trying to trace the history of its meaning backwards in the hope of figuring out what it signifies today. Exploring the changing understanding of the piece—its reception history—is another matter and a fascinating one, but that is a historical pursuit, not an interpretive one.

There is a parallel in the way language has come to be studied. Nineteenth-century and earlier linguistics was largely focused on the origin and history of words; etymology was the most important thing one could know about language. One of the insights of the late-nineteenth-century linguist Ferdinand de Saussure was that many aspects of language were much better understood by looking at how words are used now, investigating them synchronically (by a slice through time) rather than diachronically (over passing time). There is still a lot to say about a word's history, but if you want to know how it functions and is understood now, you have to look at the way it is used today. People do not speak the history of a language; they speak the language. In the same way, the present meaning of a piece of music is not something one can trace back to a work's origins (except in the historical sense of reception), not even to the composer's intent, which we can't know anyway.

The other principal fallacy of interpretation that affects music is the so-called genetic fallacy, the idea that we can discern a work's meaning by knowing the process by which it was created. This takes several forms in music, the most important being the dubious uses of the study of composers' sketches, drafts, and revisions. This kind of investigation can be brilliantly illuminating, but it is important to understand precisely what is being explicated by, say, following a composition through its creator's drafting and revision. (Beethoven, who left voluminous sketches and drafts, was the starting point for scholarship of this kind.) From this kind of study, we learn about a composer's working methods or gain insight into how a particular passage (especially one that works really well) might have sounded, which can in turn help us recognize what we like so much about the final version.

But pieces do not sound their compositional history any more than they sing their composer's intent. Knowing how a piece came to be does not tell you what it means or even how it works. And this error—the genetic fallacy—probably lies behind any attempt to understand movements of the *Mass in B Minor* by exploring their parody origins. There may be many reasons (such as the ones mentioned above) to learn about parody in Bach's music, but the uses of this knowledge are limited. We do not hear parody; we hear pieces.

And this is where the puzzle of so much writing about the *Mass in B Minor* comes in. It is difficult to understand why so much attention should be paid to the parody origin of the work or to the history of its assembly and compilation, even though these are the staples of writing about the it aimed at listeners rather than at students of Bach's working methods. It may be that the mechanics of reworking and the craftsmanship of parody are easier to grasp than problems of style, meaning, theology, and aesthetic value, making them an obvious place to turn. But we should not mistake the meaning of a *Mass* movement for whatever might have been characteristic of its reused music or for the process by which Bach transformed an older composition.

Still, there are places where our suspicion of the parody origin of a movement can call our attention to stylistic features that may have an interpretive significance. Strictly speaking, the parody process itself might not be at issue, and usually we can say that we should probably have heard and noticed these features in the first place. But the recognition of the likely parody origin of a movement can help us hear elements of the music we might not have noted. There are also a few moments in the *Mass in B Minor* in which the parody origin of a movement might be genuinely relevant to a hearing of the piece or to its meaning, passages that sound wrong against the background of eighteenth-century conventions. In them, the music sets up expectations and then foils them, particularly in formal organization, calling attention to itself. Bach may have been using these moments of frustrated expectation for compositional purposes in setting the Mass text.

A first test case might be the "Crucifixus," which every reference will tell you is a reworking of a movement from Bach's cantata "Weinen, Klagen, Sorgen, Zagen" BWV 12, composed during the time he worked at the court in Weimar (audio example 2.1a) 🔊. Bach's setting does what eighteenth-century concerted music was particularly good at: infusing a text with affect. The original movement's lamenting tone is connected to its text, "Weinen, Klagen, / Sorgen, Zagen, / Angst und Not / Sind der Christen Tränenbrot, / Die das Zeichen Jesu tragen" (Weeping, lamenting, / sorrow, fear, / anxiety, and trouble / Are the Christian's bread of tears / That bear the mark of Jesus). This tone is transferred to the Mass text, which is theologically important but neutrally reported: "Crucifixus etiam pro nobis sub Pontio Pilato, passus et sepultus est" (And he was crucified for us under Pontius Pilate, died and was buried). Bach's choice frames the plain narration of the crucifixion as a matter of sorrow as opposed to, say, awe or anger or paradoxical celebration or other possible affective interpretations.

But we would surely have known this without being told that the movement is a parody of a work with a poetic text about lamentation and tears. The "Crucifixus" is constructed over a bass line that repeats every four measures, and that line consists mostly of a descent in small musical steps (audio example 2.1b) ●. That descending bass line, presented in repetition, had been established in the early seventeenth century as an emblem of lament, starting with Claudio Monteverdi's "Lamento della ninfa," which uses a descending bass in a somewhat simpler form (audio example 2.1c) ●. You can hear the same bass Bach uses in the "Crucifixus" in Dido's lament ("When I am laid in earth") in Henry Purcell and Nahum Tate's *Dido and Aeneas* (audio example 2.1d) ● and in the opening movement of Bach's cantata "Jesu, der du meine Seele" BWV 78 (audio example 2.1e) ●, to name just two examples.

This descending bass was a conventional sign of lament. What is more, each vocal line in the "Crucifixus" opens with a so-called sighing figure (leaning onto a note that descends), another musical representation of lamentation. The musical features of the "Crucifixus" thus unmistakably mark the movement as sorrowful in eighteenth-century musical language; we do not need to know Bach's model in BWV 12 to understand that. The movement speaks for itself, as musical works almost always do. So why does every book, article, program note, or lecture tell you about the parody?

The "Crucifixus" is particularly obvious, but there are subtler connections that an awareness of parody might help us understand. The "Et in unum Dominum" is a good example. This setting of the second article of the Nicene Creed calls for two voices, and even without a deep understanding of eighteenth-century Lutheran theology, we can probably sense that Bach's use of two voices here has something to do with the text's assertion of the oneness of God as father and son ("And [I believe] in one God Jesus Christ, the only begotten son of God") (audio example 2.2a) ●. There is more here, though, and we might be pointed to the musical significance of Bach's setting by the movement's history if our ear does not catch it.

That history involves a so-called secular cantata Bach composed in 1733 to honor the son of the elector of Saxony, his ruler. The work, "Lasst uns sorgen, lasst uns wachen" BWV 213, is a drama narrating the choice between virtue and vice made by the young Hercules. (This work, which contributed many movements to the *Christmas Oratorio*, is discussed further in chapter 4.) Toward the end of the cantata, when Hercules has chosen virtue (unsurprisingly, given the obvious allegory of the royal child), the youth and personified Virtue sing a duet in which they pledge themselves to each other (audio example 2.2b) ◐. The amorous tone is obvious and the metaphor of lovers explicit, and the text opens with an unmistakable reference to the Song of Songs ("I am my beloved's and my beloved is mine"). Bach's setting, with its opening ritornello played by two solo violas matching the pair of voices, is characterized by the close intertwining of the two instrumental lines and of the two voices, part of the musical expression of the amorous quality of the text.

But this movement was not Bach's initial thought when he composed the Hercules cantata, and we know this because his autograph composing score of this movement begins with a crossed-out first attempt: a single musical line consisting of the first four measures of the music we now know as the "Et in unum Dominum" (or at least its top instrumental line). It is not clear whether Bach was copying a movement that already existed or was composing a new one on the page (probably copying), but either way, it is clear that his first thought was to set the words "Ich bin deine / Du bist meine" to the music we now know as the "Et in unum Dominum." Indeed, it is not difficult to imagine the amorous duet text with this music.

The full history here is not entirely certain; if the movement already existed at the time Bach considered using it in the Hercules cantata, then the model is lost, and the abandoned attempt to use it there and its eventual use for the "Et in unum Dominum" each derives independently from that lost work.

But that is technical history. Far more relevant to listening to the *Mass in B Minor* is the realization that the "Et in unum Dominum" bears all the markers of a love duet: paired instruments in the ritornello, paired voices, close intertwining of the vocal lines, and their unification at the ends of phrases and sections. And that, in turn, is presumably a musical expression of theological ideas in this portion of the Credo text, with the oneness of its figures metaphorically represented in amorous terms. The history of the movement, particularly the likelihood that this music served as a love duet at some point, can help us hear the characteristic features in the *Mass* version.

But as with the "Crucifixus," we do not actually need the work's likely parody status or information about its history to recognize this; a listener familiar with early-eighteenth-century musical conventions can hear the type right away. It's not that this piece was once a love duet (which it probably was, although as listeners we could not ever know that). The point here is that the movement is constructed musically like one, audibly. Do we really need parody to give us insight? No, and to invoke the parody history of the "Et in unum Dominum" as an argument in favor of hearing it this way is to inch close to the genetic fallacy. The movement calls to mind love duets not because its music once was one but rather because it sounds like one. Once again, it is not clear that parody helps us understand things about the *Mass in B Minor* that our ears were not already telling us.

Both the "Crucifixus" and the "Et in unum Dominum" are notable for their musical features representing types (repeating-bass lament and love duet) clearly audible to the experienced listener. But that is not the only way an origin in parody might make itself heard. Other movements stand out for their formal organization in ways that might best be explained by their origin in older music. This is especially true of the several choral movements constructed as ritornello forms that nonetheless lack opening ritornellos. The organization of this kind of movement is discussed in chapter 3; it depends on an opening, closing, and intermediate unit of instrumental music—the ritornello ("little thing that comes back")—whose partial or complete recurrence throughout the movement gives structure and whose musical ideas form the basis of the vocal sections between ritornello statements.

Several choral movements in the *Mass in B Minor* display all the features of a ritornello composition except the usual opening ritornello. This paradoxical organization is something heard in retrospect, of course; it takes the movement's unfolding along the lines of a ritornello piece to confirm that there was anything missing at the start. Perhaps the easiest place to hear this in the *Mass* is in the "Osanna in excelsis." At the end of the movement, after the final statement by the voices, there is a long instrumental passage (audio example 2.3a) 🔊. This is a full statement of a ritornello, recognizable by its syntax and organization. The vocal-instrumental material that precedes it shares the material of this ritornello; if your ear is attuned to such things, you can hear that the concluding statement is the only presentation of the movement's ritornello material that manages to stay in the home key rather than move from place to place harmonically. It's the stable version of material that has been presented in less stable ways throughout the movement. We expect a stable version in a ritornello-form composition but not just at the end of a piece—at the least, it belongs at the beginning, too.

If various clues point to the identity of this as a ritornello movement, where is the obligatory opening ritornello? Bach has dispensed with it, choosing to open with the voices singing "Osanna, osanna" without harmony and, in fact, without instruments (audio example 2.3b) 🔊. It seems likely that the odd formal behavior of this movement is connected with this opening, and the parody history of this movement can confirm what our ears tell us. We have evidence of two earlier forms of this music. It was probably composed for a 1732 secular cantata in which the movement began with the formulaic toast "Es lebe der König" (Long live the king). That music is lost (just the text survives), but Bach reused it for a large cantata he assembled at the last minute before a surprise 1734 visit to Leipzig by the Saxon elector and king of Poland (one and the same person). It became the first movement of the new secular cantata for the occasion, "Preise dein Glücke, gesegnetes Sachsen" BWV 215. There (and almost certainly in the lost earlier version), the movement opens with a ritornello; unsurprisingly, it is identical to the one that closes the piece both in the model and in the "Osanna in excelsis" (audio example 2.3c) 🔊. The original composition does not stop there; a somewhat contrasting section follows, and that is followed in turn by a literal repeat of the first part. This ABA structure was characteristic of settings of poetry for solo voice or for chorus; Bach reused only the A portion in the *Mass in B Minor.*

So our knowledge of the model confirms that the "Osanna in excelsis" is a ritornello form without an opening ritornello—it conventionally began with a ritornello that has been dispensed with in the *Mass*. Again, this is something we can hear from the way the movement unfolds and then ends with a closing ritornello; we don't need the model to tell us this.

In the *Mass*, there are a few other parody movements whose models survive that work the same way. The "Qui tollis peccata mundi," with no opening ritornello (audio example 2.4a) 🔊, was borrowed from the A section of the AB opening movement of the cantata "Schauet doch und sehet" BWV 46, which does have an opening ritornello. (audio example 2.4b) 🔊. The "Et expecto resurrectionem" (audio example 2.5a) 🔊 is a substantial reworking of music Bach used several times, including in the cantata "Herr Gott, Beherrscher aller Dinge"

BWV 120a; Bach used just the A section of an ABA movement, and here he removed both the opening and closing ritornellos (audio example 2.5b) ◐. The listener to the *Mass* probably does not recognize many features of ritornello form after all of Bach's surgery on the movement, but the process of adaptation is the same.

What can we learn from these movements that have lost their opening ritornellos? Bach's most important consideration appears to have been to start these movements with voices and text immediately, without an instrumental ritornello to separate the words that end one movement from the text that opens the next. This is clearly the case in the "Qui tollis peccata mundi," where Bach moves directly from the text of the "Domine Deus/Domini Fili" (audio example 2.6a; more on that transition in a moment) ◐. Opening the celebratory "Et expecto resurrectionem" immediately with voices allows Bach to contrast two settings of these words, one at the end of the "Confiteor" and one with trumpets and drums in the next movement (audio example 2.6b) ◐. The "Osanna in excelsis" opens with voices, directly following the Sanctus the first time (assuming the entire Ordinary is being performed) and after the "Benedictus" the second time (audio examples 2.6c and 2.6d) ◐.

There may be a pictorial element to the striking opening for voices alone, starting without instrumental introduction, because the words of the Sanctus are adapted from a scriptural quotation of the words of the seraphim described by Isaiah and would certainly have been recognized by the biblically literate. (The words are explicitly identified this way in Martin Luther's Sanctus hymn "Jesaia dem Propheten das geschah," heard frequently in the liturgy.) The immediate vocal entrance, without instruments, reinforces the character of these words as direct speech.

Does knowledge of the parody models for these movements, with their opening ritornellos intact, help us understand this? Not really. We can clearly hear the effect of the immediate entrance of the voices in each of these movements without knowing the models. We can recognize the vestiges of ritornello form, especially from clues such as the organization of the closing ritornello of the "Osanna in excelsis," without hearing the full versions. The parody models might make us more confident in our analysis, but our ears and knowledge of eighteenth-century conventions already tell us how these pieces depart from usual ritornello form. Perhaps our comparison of model and parody can point us to features of Bach's Mass setting, but we do not need the comparison to understand this element.

What about movements of the *Mass* that are ritornello forms and are suspected of being parodies but for which we no longer have Bach's model compositions? There are three, at least, and each begins immediately with the voices. The "Et resurrexit" is most clearly a ritornello form. It is easy to hear the so-called medial ritornello, a complete ritornello statement in the middle that is not in the home key (audio example 2.7a) 🔊, and also to hear a near-final ritornello statement that is sung and played by voices and instruments together (as is often the case in fully scored movements; in this one, a nearly complete instrumental ritornello in the home key follows, for emphasis) (audio example 2.7b) 🔊. All the markers of ritornello form are there, just without an opening ritornello. Once again, we can guess why Bach made the choice not to open the movement with instruments alone, because it lets him contrast the celebratory trumpets-and-drums setting of these words about Jesus's resurrection with the previous narration of the crucifixion and burial in the mournful "Crucifixus."

Now it is evident from Bach's autograph score that this movement is a parody, and we might even know the text to which Bach originally composed the music, depending on how confident we are that a surviving text originally belonged with it. But the model composition is lost. Did it have an opening ritornello that Bach removed in the *Mass* version? It is statistically likely that it did, because most first movements (this is one, if we are correct) have ritornellos. But we do not know, and, more important, this is about the lost model, not about the *Mass*. The "Et resurrexit" begins without a ritornello, and we don't need to know anything about its origin to hear and interpret that.

The "Et in terra pax" is probably in the same category: ritornello form, no opening ritornello, likely parody, no surviving model. And here again, Bach followed the "Gloria in excelsis Deo" immediately with the "Et in terra pax" (audio example 2.8a) 🔊. In the "Cum Sancto Spiritu," we have the same situation, in which Bach made the solo setting of the "Quoniam tu solus sanctus" lead directly into the last movement of the Gloria (audio example 2.8b) 🔊. This moment is a little different, because the "Quoniam," an aria-like ritornello form, retains its closing ritornello; the text of the "Cum Sancto Spiritu" that closes the Gloria is not heard immediately. Still, Bach appears to have wanted to keep musical momentum at the end of the entire Kyrie and Gloria setting, so he evidently avoided back-to-back ritornellos at the end of the solo movement and the start of the final chorus.

Once again, we do not really need to know about the parody origin of these movements to understand them. It is also telling that there is one ritornello choral movement in the *Mass* that has no opening ritornello but is not a parody. The "Pleni sunt coeli" section of the Sanctus is effectively an original composition; we can recall that it was taken over intact from a 1724 liturgical Sanctus setting that used precisely the same text. The "Pleni sunt coeli" never had an opening ritornello; along the conventional lines of the brief Sanctus compositions used in Lutheran central Germany, it follows the Sanctus immediately (audio example 2.8c) ◉. We can recognize elements of ritornello form in the "Pleni sunt coeli" (although this music is loose in its application of the ritornello principle) and note that it lacked an opening ritornello from the start. Parody does not figure in our analysis or listening, and there is a lesson here.

Another way the parody origin of a movement might help explain its features lies in the phrase structure of a choral movement and the ways its voices combine. There are two kinds of texts that composers tended to set chorally. The first consists of prose, usually scriptural texts; settings of this kind of text can take on many musical guises. The other consists of poetic texts, either hymn stanzas (typically incorporating a standard hymn melody) or newly written verse. This second kind, particularly in Bach's hands, tends to prompt a setting in which the organization of the poetry is clearly audible because the voices move mostly together in phrases that proceed according to the meter of the text.

A good example is the opening chorus of the *Christmas Oratorio*, "Jauchzet, frohlocket." Bach's musical setting follows the regular poetic stresses of the text; "JAUCH-zet, froh-LO-cket, auf PREI-set die TA-ge"; the strong-weak-weak dactylic meter of the poetry (German poetry is generally considered accentual rather than quantitative) is clearly audible in the music (audio example 2.9a) ◉. This is also true of the ritornello once the movement's opening fanfares are out of the way; the same metrical pattern underlies the opening instrumental presentation of this material (audio example 2.9b) ◉. A listener hearing the ritornello can guess that the movement's text will be poetic because of this regularity, and the guess is confirmed in the poetic meter clearly audible when the voices enter. If one had reason to suspect that this movement were a parody, the musically intelligent guess would be that the model was originally set to a poetic text.

In fact, the movement is a parody, and unsurprisingly, the guess is correct; the model, which survives, sets a poetic text that begins "TÖ-net, ihr PAU-ken, er-SCHAL-let Trom-PE-ten" (audio example 2.9c; there is more on this issue in chapter 4) ◉.

In setting the Mass Ordinary, Bach was faced with a prose liturgical text and looked for movements that would suit various segments of it. Some of the movements he borrowed were themselves originally settings of nonmetrical texts. For example, the "Gratias agimus tibi" and the "Dona nobis pacem" (audio examples 2.10a and 2.10b) 🔊 are based on a setting of a Psalm text that served as the first vocal movement of a church cantata for the inauguration of the Leipzig town council, "Wir danken dir, Gott, wir danken dir" BWV 29 (audio example 2.10c) 🔊. In the *Mass in B Minor*, Bach fitted this music designed for nonmetrical words with two new prose texts.

Other borrowed movements originally carried poetic texts. For example, the "Osanna in excelsis" (audio example 2.3b) 🔊, with its brief prose text, uses music that originally carried regular metrical poetry as mentioned above: "Es LE-be der KÖ-nig, der VA-ter im LAN-de," and later "PREI-se dein GLÜ-cke, ge-SEG-ne-tes SACH-sen" (audio example 2.3c) 🔊. In fact, choral movements like this were called arias in recognition of their poetic texts; the term *aria* referred to the presence of a poetic text, not to the use of a solo voice. Choral pieces were sometimes labeled "arie tutti" to acknowledge their full-ensemble settings, but they are still arias. The dactylic poetic meter of the original text is clearly audible in the music, even when it carries the prose of the "Osanna in excelsis" in the *Mass* adaptation.

This might make us suspect (if we did not already know) that the "Osanna in excelsis" is a parody, and here we might finally have an instance in which the parody origin of a movement helps us understand its musical construction. The metrical regularity that is characteristic of the vocal text setting pervades the piece. In the sung passages, the voices tend to move together as one unit, making the phrasing and meter particularly clear. Even the ritornello (heard in full, of course, only at the end) is organized throughout in regular phrases and is even more regular than the vocal setting (audio example 2.3a; try counting 1-2-3-4, with a number about every second on every strong beat, as you listen to the closing ritornello, and notice that phrases large and small all line up with this count of four) 🔊. The source of this regularity is the metrical organization of the parody model's text and would probably not have been inspired by the prose text of the *Mass* version. One could argue that in this movement, we are hearing parody.

Bach might certainly have set a prose text this way, imposing a metrical regularity on the words for musical reasons. In fact, sometimes he did do this for short texts; listen, for example, to the "Pleni sunt coeli" section of his little *Sanctus* BWV 238, which is extraordinarily regular, probably in response to the relatively regular stresses of the words (audio example 2.11a) 🔊. But the opening "Sanctus" portion of this same piece (audio example 2.11b) 🔊 is not, and it turns out that Bach did not do this often. Metrically regular settings are typically features of the settings of poetic texts, and their presence in a setting of prose stands out. (Almost all early-eighteenth-century music of this kind is organized in measures with a regular count; the characteristic feature here is the consistent way in which they group themselves in twos, fours, and eights.)

There are a few other movements in the *Mass in B Minor* in which we can hear similar hints. The opening ritornello of the "Gloria in excelsis Deo" is extraordinarily regular, breaking down into three phrases of eight measures each (audio example 2.12a) 🔊. You can easily count this out for yourself; Bach introduces subtle details to keep the movement from plodding along in identically articulated units, but it is striking how much of the movement is organized in two-, four-, and eight-measure phrases. The tendency of the voices to move together is likewise enlivened by some varied textures in which the voices enter one by one (audio example 2.12b) 🔊, but the fundamental construction of the vocal material is unified; the voices move together for the most part and clearly project the musical meter.

What do we make of these features of the "Gloria in excelsis Deo"? Commentators often describe this movement as dance-like, and the lilting triple meter and the regularity of phrasing, both conventionally (if loosely) associated with dance, contribute to this character. Those features are also closely associated with settings of poetic texts, and a reasonable conclusion is that this music was originally composed for one. We are probably hearing the musical organization that resulted from Bach's reuse of this music for prose; we are hearing a parody. Other movements in the *Mass in B Minor* also point in this direction, including the "Et resurrexit," whose ritornello is not quite so periodic but whose vocal declamation suggests a metrically regular text in its history.

We can see how complicated this is, though, by thinking about the "Et expecto resurrectionem" (audio example 2.5a) 🔊. The organization of this music does not so obviously suggest poetic meter, but a look at the surviving parody model (the opening movement of "Herr Gott, Beherrscher aller Dinge" BWV 120a) reveals that the movement was composed to a poetic text (audio example 2.5b) 🔊. In that setting, though, Bach deemphasized the metrical regularity of the poem in favor of a much freer setting; this made it ideal for adaptation to the prose Mass text. There is demonstrably parody at work in the "Et expecto resurrectionem," but it is not really audible. (If you listen to the rest of that model from BWV 120a—the *Mass* uses only the A section of an ABA setting—you will hear that even though the outer A sections do not emphasize the poetic organization of the text, the middle B section definitely does; audio example 2.5c) 🔊.

Parody might also explain oddities of scoring in the *Mass in B Minor*. One especially puzzling passage is the "Et iterum venturus est" section of the "Et resurrexit." For the words "et iterum venturus est cum gloria judicare vivos et mortuos" (and he will come again with glory to judge the living and the dead), the full ensemble of voices and instruments (including trumpets and drums) is reduced to the vocal bass line, basso continuo, and a sparse harmonic accompaniment in the strings (audio example 2.13a) 🔊. The passage is particularly baffling in modern performances that employ a large chorus, where the sudden shift to "solo" composition appears to be without motivation (audio example 2.13b) 🔊, to say nothing of the strange effect when this extended passage is sung by the entire choral bass section, as is often heard (audio example 2.13c) 🔊. What is going on, and does parody play a role in our understanding of the movement?

It is likely that this piece is a parody of the opening movement of a cantata whose music is lost that Bach composed for a royal birthday, "Entfernet euch, ihr heitern Sterne" BWV Anh. 9. A printed text survives, and there are enough clues in the *Mass* version to suggest that this lost composition was the model. That work was a musical drama delivered by named mythological and allegorical characters (Phyliris, Apollo, Mars, and Harmony), each sung by one singer, as you would expect. They combined in an "aria tutti" at the beginning and the end, retaining their identities as individual characters but also functioning as a single musical ensemble (the chorus). The model for the "Et resurrexit" was probably the opening aria tutti of the drama, and the solo passage in the first movement that would later bear the "Et iterum" text ("Die Gluth des Himmel-reinsten Flammen . . .") was probably sung by Mars, who would conventionally have been represented by a bass voice.

There are similar moments in other works by Bach, for example, an extended passage for solo bass in the last movement of "Lasst uns sorgen, lasst uns wachen," the Hercules drama. (audio example 2.14a and 2.14b) 🔊. This movement is in the voice of the "Chorus of the Muses," additional to the mythological and allegorical characters who appear elsewhere in the piece but almost certainly sung by the same vocalists who sang those characters, with one voice on each line. This is one of the only movements from the Hercules cantata that Bach did not reuse in the *Christmas Oratorio*, although there is some evidence that he originally planned to; if he had, there its scoring might have closely resembled the "Et resurrexit" with its solo bass interlude.

Does the sudden appearance of the solo passage in the "Et resurrexit" of the *Mass* point to parody? It makes sense that there might be a parody explanation for this surprising change in vocal scoring, but given that this kind of writing does appear in eighteenth-century music (for example, in Bach's own Hercules cantata), there is no reason it could not have been original to a Mass setting. Once again, I am not certain that the knowledge of a likely parody helps here, even though we have gotten in the habit of invoking it, because it is possible that this musical feature, though unexpected, is original to the piece, not the accidental result of reworking.

There are also a few places in the *Mass in B Minor* where strange formal things happen; the listener is given every cue that a piece will go in a particular direction, only to find that it does not, instead violating well-established conventions. We have grown accustomed to the *Mass* versions, but in conventional terms, these movements in which formal expectations are raised and then disappointed are exceptional. Is parody the explanation here?

The best example is the "Domine Deus/Domini Fili," a soprano 1-tenor duet with transverse flute, strings, and basso continuo, and the striking moment is the sudden appearance of the choral setting of "Qui tollis peccata mundi" without a break (audio example 2.15a) 🔊. This is unexpected because the listener has been given many cues that suggest that something different and more conventional was about to happen.

The piece is constructed in the manner of a duet aria, although Bach did not call it an aria because it is not a setting of a poetic text. It has a long opening ritornello, a sort of false start for the voices, an extended vocal section after the "real" vocal beginning, and, most important, a return of the opening ritornello in the home key. These features are all conventional, and together they signal to a listener familiar with early-eighteenth-century vocal music that this will be a particular kind of piece with a specific formal organization. What happens next confirms this: at the end of the ritornello, instead of a stop, we get a continuation of the piece, the reentrance of the voices on a new segment of text ("Domine Deus, Agnus Dei") in a setting that is somewhat contrasting with what has gone before.

These gestures all point to the most common kind of solo aria, in which an A section (framed by ritornellos) is followed by a B section that might introduce some contrasting elements and often goes twice through its part of the text. Then comes a literal return of A, usually complete with its ritornellos, with the opening text again. Almost every opera aria in the early eighteenth century was constructed this way, as was a large proportion of arias in Bach's liturgical music. For example, many of the arias in the *Christmas Oratorio* are organized this way, and two behave precisely like the "Domine Deus/Domini Fili." In the aria "Grosser Herr, o starker König," for example, an opening ritornello is followed by a long vocal segment, then rounded off with the ritornello again; this is the A section (audio example 2.15b) ◐. A somewhat contrasting section follows that presents two vocal statements of the next lines of the text beginning "Der die ganze Welt erhält," separated by an instrumental ritornello.

This is the B section, and its close is particularly telling. The instruments drop out, leaving just the voice and basso continuo to make a cadence. This sets up the return of the complete A section (ritornello, vocal segment, ritornello) to round off the piece. The shorthand name for this kind of ABA piece is *da capo aria; da capo* means "from the top" and refers to the complete return of A, in which performers are told literally to look back to the start of the movement on the page and play the A section again from the same notation.

That moment at the end of B, with characteristic harmonic features and the withdrawal of the instruments (here trumpet and strings) is also heard, among many examples, in the aria "Schlafe, mein Liebster" from the *Christmas Oratorio* (audio example 2.15c) ◐. The aria has an opening ritornello, goes twice through the first part of its text ("Schlafe, mein Liebster") with a ritornello in between, then closes with a return of the opening ritornello. All this represents A. The next lines of text, "Labe die Brust," occupy the B section, and once again the cadence of B is formed by voice and continuo, without the strings and oboes. That is the signal for the return to the beginning and a re-statement of A. (Bach doubles the voice throughout with transverse flute; it participates in that cadence at the end of B, but the main group of instruments is withdrawn.) Many musical features—the structure of the A section, the organization of contrasting B material, and the handling of the vocal cadence—all announce where we are and what will happen next, even when we hear the aria for the first time.

With these examples in your ear, you can recognize, as an experienced eighteenth-century listener would, that the same thing happens in the "Domine Deus/Domini Fili" in the *Mass in B Minor*. The cadence after its two statements of the second half of the text ("Domine Deus, Agnus Dei") is set up and made in the same way; everything that happens tells us to expect a return to the start, to the ritornello, to the home key, and to the opening text (audio example 2.15d) 🔊. Bach gives every signal, but the outcome is foiled. With the appearance of the text "Qui tollis peccata mundi," we get a new text, a new musical meter, an entirely new vocal and instrumental texture, and the wrong key.

This leaves the "Domine Deus/Domini Fili" incomplete; it never returns to its home key, as almost every movement in the work (and essentially every piece of this da capo type) does. The "Qui tollis peccata mundi" that follows has its problems, too, including the fact that it starts and ends in different keys, neither of which is the key of the duet it follows. (You might not be surprised to learn that the "Qui tollis peccata mundi" is one of those recycled ritornello movements without its opening ritornello.)

Altogether, there are many things in this moment of the Gloria that invite interpretation: the lack of key closure of the "Domine Deus/Domini Fili," the lack of key closure of the "Qui tollis peccata mundi," the lack of key closure of this pair of connected movements, and the decision to connect them in the first place. There is no missing the wrong turn at the end of the duet for someone familiar with eighteenth-century conventions, and it appears that Bach wanted listeners to note the arrival of the "Qui tollis peccata mundi" in this way (harmonically, thematically, and texturally unexpected), given that he provides every clue to the piece's structure and to the return of the duet's A section and the opening text but then denies this outcome.

Once again, the question is whether we attempt to explain this by recourse to parody. There are many reasons to suspect that Bach created this effect by the adaptation of an extant duet, and to think that the model was probably a da capo piece that behaved normally, with a return of the A section at the expected place. We know that the "Qui tollis peccata mundi" is a parody of the opening chorus of the cantata "Schauet doch und sehet" BWV 46, which lost its opening ritornello in the *Mass* version, allowing the "Qui tollis" text to follow immediately on the end of the previous duet. Parody is a handy explanation here and even offers the possibility that the duet points self-consciously to its origin and reworking.

Once again, though, we can ask whether we need parody to understand this moment. The end of the "Domine Deus/Domini Fili" surely foils our expectations, and as students of this music and its history, we know that this probably stemmed from the parody and truncation of a formally ordinary piece. But consider a parallel example in which Bach appears to have played on a closely related convention in an original composition: the aria "Ich ende behände mein irdisches Leben" from near the end of the cantata *Selig ist der Mann* BWV 57 (audio example 2.15e) 🔊. In his setting, Bach treats the text in a way that makes us expect a return of the opening material. This is not set up as a strict ABA movement, but we are led to expect a return to the home key and a closing ritornello, and probably a return of the opening text. There is none; Bach leaves things entirely up in the air and in the wrong key, ending with the voice on a very weakly asserted cadence.

There is a reason. The aria is from a cantata for St. Stephen's Day (the second day of Christmas) and alludes to that saint's being taken up suddenly into heaven. The first part of the aria text says, "I quickly end my earthly life / I long to depart just now with joy," and the unexpected and musically interrupting close of the aria has obvious interpretive meaning. But if Bach could do this in an original work—that is, manipulate a formal convention of arias to generate meaning—could he not also do this in a Mass movement? It might be difficult to say precisely why he led the "Domine Deus/Domini Fili" directly into the "Qui tollis peccata mundi" in an unexpected way, but we do not really need the parody origin of the two movements to notice and appreciate the gesture.

Historians and analysts have tended to favor approaches to the *Mass in B Minor* that start with its undeniable parody origins, both when we have the models and when we do not, and have tended to explain unconventional moments as byproducts of the parody process. But listeners in Bach's time and ours could not be expected to know the parody models. What is more, most of the features that have typically been explained by parody make musical sense on their own, without recourse to the hidden and mostly inaudible history of the work. The occasional mismatch of a musical style designed for poetry set to prose words might be the single exception. Other than that, parody appears to be overrated as a starting point for appreciating the *Mass*. We are probably better off beginning with what we can hear as we try to understand this music.

THREE

The Musical Topic of the *Mass in B Minor*

Can a musical work be about something?

If European art music of the nineteenth century had a collective obsession, it was with the questions of whether music could convey extramusical meaning, how it might do so, and (debated most vehemently) whether it should properly try in the first place. The era's fascination with musical meaning can be seen in the vast repertory of so-called programmatic music—instrumental works with extramusical narratives, characters, or ideas. It also made itself felt in various kinds of opera whose ideals involved the musical communication of drama instrumentally as well as vocally.

Although there was an aesthetic turn in the twentieth century away from meaning in favor of a tendency to value objectivity and abstractness, the obsession with meaning never went away, particularly because of the continued museum-like cultivation of music for orchestra, chamber ensembles, and piano inherited from the nineteenth century. Along with that repertory, we have inherited many of the century's ideas about what it means to say that a piece of music means something—is about something—to the extent that the question "What is this piece about?" more or less inevitably points in the direction of extramusical meaning and significance. You might even be tempted to ask in reply, "What else could it be about? Itself?"

That approach makes sense for the repertory of the nineteenth century, but what happens when we turn the question on a work from the early eighteenth? What is a work by Bach about? This is much harder to answer but mostly does not involve extramusical factors. To be sure, there had been a continuous tradition since the late sixteenth century of works that narrated or imitated or depicted, and a few eighteenth-century compositions are about things in this sense. (For an example by Bach, listen to his narrative work for keyboard known as the *Capriccio on the Departure of a Most Beloved Brother* BWV 992.) But pieces like these were understood to represent a special category in which music attempted something it ordinarily did not. Works of music were not routinely about something extramusical.

Sometimes pieces referred to musical types that carried extramusical associations, such as music of the hunt, military marches, or idealized pastoral music, corresponding to what analysts of later eighteenth-century music have come to call topics. (For example, a symphony movement by Franz Joseph Haydn might take up the musical topic of a march without claiming to be one literally.) But an early-eighteenth-century composition that borrowed the characteristic horn calls of hunt music—a concerto, for example—was not necessarily about the hunt; it simply took its stereotyped musical sounds as a starting point (audio example 3.1) 🔊.

So what were eighteenth-century pieces about, if anything? There is no simple answer, and in fact, philosophers of the new field of musical aesthetics devoted a lot of thought to what music was for, how it worked, and what it was about. In the middle of the century, Jean-Jacques Rousseau famously quoted Bernard de Fontenelle's question "Sonata, what do you want of me?" evidently as an expression of uncertainty and even frustration in coming to terms with instrumental music. Part of his exasperation probably came from nagging questions about what music might be trying to do besides sound nice or sometimes evoke sublime awe, especially as the longstanding goal of moving a listener's affections began to fade in importance.

The situation might seem a little better with vocal music equipped with text; indeed, Fontenelle's question is specifically addressed to the sonata, typically an abstract piece of purely instrumental music. Of course, there were vocal works with text about hunting that invoked the musical hunt type, but the relationship between music and meaning is different in pieces like this; a texted work is presumably about its text. But the more one thinks about that statement, the less it appears to say. This becomes particularly evident when you consider texts such as the Ordinary of the Mass (the text of the *Mass in B Minor*) that were set over and over. If they are about their text, are all Mass settings about the same thing? From a liturgical point of view, they might be, although various settings might present different views of the fixed words.

Even with the gaps in our knowledge, we can be reasonably certain that Bach's lengthy setting of the complete Mass was not a practical liturgical work, so its potential meaning in relation to the liturgy is at least a step removed. It might reflect and even express its text or the theological ideas behind it, but in that regard, it is no different from any contemporary setting—it is difficult to see that it makes a striking and individual statement.

In fact, the *Mass in B Minor* might be a particularly good candidate as an eighteenth-century musical work that is about something other than its function or the specific meaning of its text, precisely because it does not appear to have been created with practical use in mind in the way that even the *St. Matthew Passion* was. I think the subject of the *Mass in B Minor* is musical. The work self-consciously explores a musical problem that was central to composition in the first half of the eighteenth century.

The problem concerns musical style. *Style* is a loose term nowadays; it can apply to fashion (shoes in the latest style); to an individual, musical or otherwise (Grace Kelly's style, Antonio Vivaldi's style); or to a way of doing almost anything. As a teacher of mine is fond of pointing out, you can order "eggs any style" in a diner. Actually, that example may come closest to the seventeenth- and eighteenth-century musical understanding of the word *style* because it refers to a way of doing something (poaching, frying, etc.). The origins of the word are literary and refer to the very act of writing, as with a stylus. The concept took on this meaning in music, too, pointing to different ways of composing, literally of writing music.

This musical sense of style did not usually refer to specific composers the way we often use it (Bach's style, Georg Philipp Telemann's style) but rather to the kind of writing appropriate to pieces of various types and functions. This, in turn, owed a great deal to seventeenth-century musical thinkers' fascination with the kinds of music in their world, with its classification in rational and scientific terms, and with its characterization. There were schemes of high and low styles, modern and old styles, strict and free styles, and styles designated by place of musical performance (church, theater, or chamber). Each musical style was characterized by particular kinds of writing thought to be proper and characteristic. Pieces of music, by their construction, announced their musical style and appropriate performance context, even when they borrowed styles and transplanted them from from one context to a foreign one. They did this by the various ways in which they were written, with *written* (implying notation) standing in for the act of composing. Music moved from one context to another, carrying its stylistic significance with it.

By the time Bach assembled the *Mass in B Minor*, the concept of style helped musicians come to terms with a particular feature of early-eighteenth-century church music: that there were two ecclesiastical styles. One was old-fashioned and fundamentally vocal, borrowing and adapting the compositional technique of Giovanni Pierluigi da Palestrina, his sixteenth-century contemporaries, and his seventeenth-century imitators. This is a musical style understood to have been proper to the church from the start, rarely if ever transplanted to other contexts in the eighteenth century for reasons of propriety; when it was heard elsewhere, particularly the chamber, it often connoted learnedness rather than religiosity. The other ecclesiastical style was modern and drew on up-to-date music such as the instrumental concerto and the opera aria, representing stylistic transplants from the chamber and the theater to the church.

Both kinds of writing came to be appropriate to church music, but each represented a different style in the strict sense of the term, and they were viewed as being opposed in some senses. They could exist side by side, and indeed, musicians continued to compose and perform music in the old style (both genuine old pieces and imitations of them that incorporated some aspects of modern musical language) and to cultivate church music that incorporated the most up-to-date techniques. The two styles could also be combined, both for contrast in distinct movements of larger works and in attempts to reconcile them within a single movement.

If there is a fundamental musical topic of Bach's *Mass in B Minor*, it is the existence of these two styles appropriate to church music that employed both voices and instruments and the tension between them. The movements that make up the *Mass* can be read as presenting the entire spectrum of possibilities offered by the modern and antique styles, ranging from movements purely in one or the other to a dazzling variety of ways of reconciling and combining the two with different balances.

From this point of view, the topic of the *Mass* is musical style itself. This has been expressed in other ways, including (for example) the nice formulation that the *Mass* represents a "specimen book" or sampler of musical types and styles. I would go a step further and say that the piece systematically explores a particular stylistic problem. It does not simply lay out the range of musical styles available to the church composer (although it does that, including in the Kyrie and Gloria, which Bach originally presented to the Dresden court in 1733, presumably as a demonstration of his abilities in all kinds of music). It goes further, looking for points of contact between the two styles and exploring the possibilities of their reconciliation.

This is surely not the only thing the *Mass in B Minor* is about, but it does offer an eighteenth-century way of listening to the piece, with an awareness of fundamental issues of musical style and composition. And it might help explain some of Bach's compositional choices, including one that has long intrigued listeners: why he repeated the music of the "Gratias agimus tibi" for the work's closing setting of the words "Dona nobis pacem."

One way to learn to hear the work this way is to examine movements at opposite ends of the stylistic spectrum—pieces entirely in the old and new styles—as points of reference. The purest example of the older style in the *Mass* is the "Confiteor." Most important, all of its musical material is in its vocal lines. There is no independent role for instruments (leaving aside the basso continuo, to which we will return). This is particularly striking in a work like the *Mass in B Minor*, whose essence lies in its combination of voices and instruments. It is a so-called concerted work, meaning (in the eighteenth century) a composition that did precisely that. There was plenty of church music that used only voices and continuo—mostly pieces in the old style—but in a multimovement concerted work like the *Mass*, the composer had to make a conscious choice to omit an independent role for the instruments, as in the "Confiteor."

A catch: in some performances, instruments do play in this movement. The matter is discussed in some detail in chapter 1, but the short version is that even though Bach did not specify instrumental participation in this movement in the only surviving source, we know from his documented performances of other music that in movements of this kind, he typically had instruments play along, doubling the voices. This is worth reflecting on, because it represents a completely different kind of collaboration of voices and instruments from those in most of the rest of the *Mass* or in Bach's cantatas or in his Passion settings. In most movements of those other works (aside from the simplest declamatory recitatives and hymn harmonizations), we are justified in hearing instruments as the dominant musical element, with voices embedded in an instrumental texture. Voices and their roles are adapted to an instrumental context that largely governs harmony, the construction of musical phrases, and many other elements.

Old-style movements such as the "Confiteor" work the other way around. This is music designed for voices to which instruments can be added for reinforcement, playing precisely what the voices sing. The writing is idiomatically vocal: range is limited; text is declaimed in a simple way, often with one note for each syllable; and the speed of text declamation is steady and relatively constant. It makes no use of the idiomatic things that strings or woodwinds or brass instruments are capable of: virtuosity, elaborate ornamentation of musical lines, extremes of range, or almost anything else characteristic of instrumental writing.

With the domination of vocal writing goes another feature closely associated with the old style, and it concerns the relationship of the vocal lines (soprano 1, soprano 2, alto, tenor, and bass in the "Confiteor") to one another. That relationship is contrapuntal. That is, each line is a satisfying melodic line on its own, and the substance of the piece arises from the interaction of the five independent lines, note against note ("punct contra punct" in the roots of the term). You can contrast this way of using voices to the way they are employed in a simple chorale harmonization at the end of many church cantatas by Bach. In these settings, the voices move mostly together; with the possible exception of the soprano line, where the familiar hymn tune resides, the lines are not meant to be heard individually but rather as a group forming the substance of the piece. In a contrapuntal piece, you are meant to hear the individual lines and their combination into a musical texture.

That contrapuntal relationship is made more audible by the pervasive use of a particular compositional technique that emphasizes the voices' simultaneous independence and interconnectedness. At the beginning of the "Confiteor" and at a series of moments in it, the musical substance begins with one voice and then systematically adds the others one by one until there is a full five-voice texture (audio example 3.2a) 🔊. The staggered entrances point to the independence of each line; the interconnectedness comes from the fact that each voice enters with the same material, imitating the voices that started before. The musical texture thus arises from the simultaneous presentation of overlapping statements of the same (or closely similar) material.

In fact, this technique of imitation, repeated for each grammatical phrase of a text, was the fundamental constructive module of old-fashioned vocal polyphony (music made up of contrapuntally related voices), which typically proceeded phrase by phrase through the text, treating each phrase in imitative counterpoint before reaching some kind of close and starting with new imitation on the next segment of text. After the first imitative setting of the words "Confiteor unum baptisma," for example, the voices reach a cadence (a close), then enter one by one on a new idea in slightly faster notes on the next segment of the text, "in remissionem peccatorum" (audio example 3.2b) 🔊. This is typical of old-style pieces.

At this point (after settings of the phrases beginning "Confiteor" and "in remissionem"), Bach has gotten all the way through his text, but he does not end the movement here. Instead, he extends the piece by returning to those two units of text simultaneously (audio example 3.2c) 🔊. It turns out that the musical ideas he has invented for each of the two textual phrases can be combined. The five voices enter two at a time in various combinations, simultaneously presenting the two phrases set to their musical subjects. He follows the same impulse by next showing that the subject setting "Confiteor" can be imitated in a different way, with the voices entering far more quickly one after the other than the first time; this represents another contrapuntal insight into the possibilities of this material, perhaps the musical ability for which Bach is best known. This demonstration of contrapuntal virtuosity is more a feature of eighteenth-century music than sixteenth-, so it represents a somewhat modern touch within the contrapuntal spirit of the old style. But it is telling in its emphasis on a characteristic feature of the old style: its contrapuntal construction.

Bach is still not through pursuing old style in this movement. He returns to the combination of the musical ideas associated with "Confiteor" and "in remissionem," showing that they can be combined in still further ways. But more strikingly, he adds another old-fashioned (even antique) element by introducing the chant melody used in the Lutheran church for the words "Confiteor unum baptisma," embedding the preexistent tune in slow notes in the contrapuntal texture (audio example 3.2d) 🔊. This is a very old technique known as *cantus firmus*. Bach further shows off his abilities by having the chant appear in two voices with entries staggered so that the two statements of the chant overlap and create their own imitative counterpoint with each other, in the manner of a round. Then (we are still not done) Bach introduces the same chant melody in even slower notes in another voice, making the cantus firmus texture particularly audible and reinforcing the old-fashioned musical approach (audio example 3.2e) 🔊.

It is essential to note that Bach's construction of the "Confiteor" has little to do with the meaning of the text at the level of words and phrases or with its affective (emotional) elements. The focus is rather on musical artifice, counterpoint, and constructive techniques—on contrapuntal imitation, the combination of musical subjects, the presentation of a chant tune as a cantus firmus embedded in the texture.

This is entirely characteristic of the old style as it was cultivated in the early eighteenth century, because that style was considered fundamentally affect-neutral; it did not aim to move the affections (emotional states) of the listener in the way modern styles did.

This neutrality (affectively speaking) made the style particularly well suited to texts such as the "Confiteor." The "confession of baptism in remission of sin" is as abstract a concept as one can imagine, important to the believer but a matter of doctrine largely without affective character. Bach's choice of the old style here in its purest form indicates his presentation of this portion of the text as doctrinal. (Just contrast the ecstatic dance with trumpets and drums suggested by the opening of the "Gloria in excelsis Deo.") Actually, one does not have to look any further than the continuation of this movement itself to hear the difference. After presenting the words beginning "Confiteor," the *Mass in B Minor* continues with two settings of the text "et expecto resurrectionem mortuorum," one with the same vocal forces as in the "Confiteor" and one with the full vocal and instrumental apparatus including trumpets and drums (audio examples 3.3a and 3.3b) 🜂.

Each of these is deeply affective in contrasting ways; the compositional focus in both is on emotional character. This is a principal difference between the old and new church styles. The former was fundamentally neutral, the latter focused on the moving of the listener's affections. (Note that at the turn to an affective presentation, the "Confiteor" abandons its old-style imitative counterpoint and takes up simultaneous declamation by the voices.)

There are a few features of this very old-fashioned "Confiteor" setting that mark it as belonging to the eighteenth century and not the sixteenth. It includes a basso continuo part, as did essentially every piece in Bach's time. Here the continuo line is a so-called walking bass almost entirely in steadily moving notes. This was not a part of ancient polyphony but became a stereotyped way to accompany eighteenth-century imitations of the style. In the *Mass in B Minor*, you can hear it again in the "Credo in unum Deum," a movement also in a (slightly extended) old style and likewise presenting a doctrinal statement (audio example 3.4) 🜂. The contrapuntal combination of two musical subjects ("Confiteor" and "in remissionem") owes more to modern fugue than to old-style vocal polyphony, and the harmonic language of the piece is definitely eighteenth-century. But all the markers of old style are evident.

There is even one old-fashioned feature that relates literally to style as a way of writing. The musical notation of this movement is antiquated, using symbols in ways that recall notation from the sixteenth century. Most obvious is the use of symbols that usually represented slow notes as the basic pulse. Only a performer or someone studying the score would be aware of the notation, but we shouldn't underestimate the power of this sort of stylistic cue, which has a close parallel in typography and spelling. Imagine reading this passage from the King James translation of a verse from Genesis aloud: "𝔄𝔫𝔡 𝔊𝔬𝔡 𝔰𝔞𝔦𝔡: 𝔏𝔢𝔱 𝔱𝔥𝔢𝔯𝔢 𝔟𝔢 𝔩𝔦𝔤𝔥𝔱: 𝔞𝔫𝔡 𝔱𝔥𝔢𝔯𝔢 𝔴𝔞𝔰 𝔩𝔦𝔤𝔥𝔱." All the words are familiar and even spelled precisely as in modern English, but on the page, the typeface almost certainly connotes age or even antiquity and maybe even brings a whiff of the church itself. Its appearance might tempt you to read it in a particularly authoritative voice. Someone listening to you, though, would have no idea how the text was printed. This is what the musical notation of the "Confiteor" suggests, not only communicating the movement's antiquated style but also potentially alerting performers to roles they might play in its performance. This especially affected the instrumentalists, who double the voices rather than having their own material as they would in a modern movement notated in a modern way.

Bach was exposed to sixteenth-century vocal polyphony in his younger years, but he also returned to it later; much of the evidence of his performance and composition of music that emulates Palestrina and his contemporaries dates from late in his life. We know that Bach owned a manuscript score copy of six Mass settings by Palestrina himself, and we have a set of performing parts (made in later years) for the Kyrie and Gloria of one of them, a six-part composition, pointing to a performance of this music under Bach's direction (audio examples 3.5a and 3.5b) 🔊. Characteristically, Bach added a basso continuo part and doubled the voices with cornetto and trombones, instruments strongly associated with old-style church music. This piece is notable more for a rich texture generated from short, overlapping vocal entrances than from drawn-out imitation and self-conscious counterpoint, but there is no mistaking it for a modern piece. Bach and an assistant also began preparing performing parts for another four-voice Mass from this collection but broke off partway through the preparation of doubling instrumental parts. This work uses a chant cantus firmus, as in Bach's "Confiteor." Another Mass in the collection employs a chant cantus firmus presented in canonic imitation, in overlapping statements in two voices, just as in the "Confiteor."

The *Mass in B Minor* includes one other movement in more or less pure old style: the second "Kyrie eleison" (audio example 3.6) 🔊. You can recognize many of the features it shares with the "Confiteor": musical material confined to the voices, with instruments relegated to doubling; polyphonic construction focusing on the individual melodic identity of each of the vocal lines (four in this movement); pervasive imitation of one part by the next as the organizing principle; sectional construction, beginning afresh with just one voice several times; and a musical subject that is confined to an idiomatically vocal narrow range. These features all point to old style, and you will not be surprised to learn that this movement, too, is presented in old-fashioned notation.

But there are also some modern features of the second "Kyrie eleison." For a start, the musical subject on which the movement is based has the contours and rhythms of a sixteenth-century idea but uses notes from outside the principal scale employed in the movement; its slinky character marks it as belonging to the eighteenth century. (I think Bach has a purpose here, but we will return to that later.) Also characteristic of Bach and of modern times is the composer's exploration of all the contrapuntal possibilities of his subject in an exhaustive process over the course of the movement. Even more than the "Confiteor," this movement focuses mostly on one musical idea throughout; that is an eighteenth-century procedure, not a sixteenth-century one, whatever the outward appearance of the movement. There is a basso continuo line here, too, of course; it sometimes tends toward the walking-bass type heard in the "Confiteor" but sometimes participates as though it were another voice in the contrapuntal texture (and sometimes doubles the bass vocal line). This, too, is a modern adaptation, but the pointers to old style are unambiguous.

The "Confiteor" and the "Kyrie eleison II" are the two movements in Bach's *Mass in B Minor* that best represent pure old style, contrasted with pieces in the modern style, which greatly outnumber them. One of the most characteristic of those is the "Laudamus te," which could not be farther from the movements modeled on sixteenth-century vocal works. First is its scoring: a solo violin, ensemble strings, basso continuo, and solo voice—heterogeneous where the old-style movements are uniform, offering a variety of colors and mixing voices and instruments given characteristic and independent material to play. This movement divides its presentation of musical material between instruments and voice rather than being a fundamentally vocal piece.

The violin line (audio example 3.7a) ◉ is florid, ornamented, virtuosic, and idiomatic to the instrument. It is only barely singable, certainly not in the way that the material of the old-style movements is. Its very conception is connected to instrumental performance, not to vocal ideals. In fact, the movement is easier to understand as an instrumentally conceived work with the participation of a voice, even though we have gotten in the habit of thinking of movements like it in Bach's concerted vocal music as vocal pieces with instrumental "accompaniment." Listen to the vocal entrance, and recognize the level of virtuosic singing it takes to echo the material presented by the violin (audio example 3.7b) 🎵.

The solo violin melody (and it is a tune, not just a short idea designed to set a phrase of text compactly, as in the "Confiteor") is set against an accompanying line in the basso continuo in a relationship that might be called polarized. The violin line dominates, supported by the bass line. The ensemble strings are subordinate, enriching the texture and reinforcing specific moments. Overall, the relationships among the participants are very different from the equality among voices in the old-style pieces. There is a hierarchy of predominating melody (solo violin and sometimes voice), accompanying bass line, and reinforcing ensemble strings and a clear differentiation of material and roles in the musical texture. This is the opposite of the old-style movements, where the contrapuntal independence of each line and the shared imitative material suggest an equality of parts. In fact, that kind of piece is sometimes called equal-voice polyphony; the lines are differentiated by range (soprano, alto, tenor, bass) but equal in status. In the "Confiteor," the roles are adjusted only for the presentation of a chant cantus firmus, where one or two voices are distinguished; in the "Laudamus te," the distinctness of musical lines is part of the design.

The violin's opening passage, before the entrance of the voice, extends for a long stretch of musical time, far longer than that covered by the imitated subject in the "Confiteor" and even considerably longer than the time it takes for all the voices to enter with that subject. The important point here is not the length of the musical phrase itself but what makes it long, and the answer is a completely different kind of musical syntax compared with the "Confiteor." The violin line in the "Laudamus te" is far more goal-oriented, heading for a series of intermediate cadences (arrival points) and ultimately a final one before the entrance of the voice. It presents several musical ideas of different kinds, varying in rhythm, melodic shape, and many other parameters. It chains together small musical ideas repeated on successively higher or lower pitches, turning repetition (technically, "sequences") into a constructive element. And although it is not fully regular, it has many passages of balanced phrases that echo or answer what came before. We can contrast all these features with the vocal lines in the "Confiteor," which do none of these things; they are musical prose compared with the poetry of the "Laudamus te."

The opening instrumental passage has a characteristic overall organization, too, which is very different from anything in the "Confiteor." It presents opening material, then comes to a pause, alighting for a moment's repose; then makes a kind of digression as it presents some new ideas in sequential repetition (that is, melodically repetitive but on successively higher or lower pitches); then it builds to a cadence. (In most recordings, that first moment of repose comes about twenty seconds in; at about forty seconds into the piece, you can hear the drive toward the cadence.) This is a stereotyped pattern—opening idea, a spinning out, and a cadence—that characterizes most of the *Mass in B Minor*'s modern-style movements.

This musical segment matters a great deal, in fact, because it forms, in turn, the constructive unit of the entire movement. Statements of this musical unit, in part or in full, appear in the instruments throughout the piece, alternating with vocal passages. The returning instrumental material frames the work, appearing at the beginning and again at the end and at structural moments throughout. In the "Laudamus te," it returns after the first vocal section (about 1:45 in typical recordings, audio example 3.7c) 🔊, again after a second vocal section (at about 2:30, audio example 3.7d) 🔊, and at the end (audio example 3.7e) 🔊. None of these other statements is complete, but we recognize them by their musical material and by the participation of all the instruments. (It was conventional to have a complete restatement of the material at the end in this kind of movement, but composers sometimes decided to abbreviate the last return, as Bach does here, probably because it was somewhat redundant by that point after all the other statements.)

What I am describing here was a basic construction familiar from both early-eighteenth-century concertos and opera arias. It is known as ritornello form after the Italian term for a little unit (of music) that returns, a *ritornello*. The governing principle is that a ritornello invented by the composer comes back several times in full or in part; between statements of it come either solo instrumental material (in a concerto) or vocal material (in an aria or a piece constructed like one). Bach started composing ritornello movements of this type (both vocal and instrumental) in the 1710s and was particularly influenced by the music of Vivaldi as he learned to construct pieces in this way. It is worth noting that the focus of musical attention in this kind of piece—the thing that makes one concerto different from another or one aria distinct from the next—is that a ritornello rarely comes back literally except at the end. Rather, it almost appears shortened or harmonically transformed or both. The harmonic transformation, particularly by moving the ritornello to a higher or lower pitch and directing it to a musical close centered on some note other than the piece's home pitch, is what makes the piece seem to progress from place to place (metaphorically speaking) and then return home as the ritornello reappears in its original form at its original pitch.

It is worth trying to listen to the "Laudamus te" from this point of view, as a ritornello piece that is fundamentally about statements and returns of the ritornello played by the solo violin and ensemble strings. To do this, you need to ignore the voice, which is pretty much the opposite of the way most people approach movements like this. The "Laudamus te" is only about four minutes long in most performances, so this is an experiment worth trying, because it offers an eighteenth-century approach to the construction of the piece—at least, a musician's approach. That is not to claim that nobody listened to the singer or the text; the point is that the basis of the piece was understood by composers and technical writers about pieces like this to be the instrumental ritornello.

If you do listen in this way, you might notice a particular feature of the movement. At several points while the voice is singing, the solo violin and ensemble strings enter with a simultaneous statement of the ritornello, particularly its characteristic opening gesture and sometimes also its continuation. In these places, you can hear that that the vocal line is simply fit into instrumental statements of ritornello material; it does not lead or dominate but is melodically subordinate. This is striking when you think about it, because modern listeners typically think of the instruments as supporting the voice, not that the vocal line sometimes fits into instrumental passages where it can.

If the musical material of this movement is idiomatically instrumental; and if instrumental statements begin, end, and articulate the piece; and if the vocal line sometimes is simply embedded into instrumental ritornello material, we can ask whether this sort of piece (and the opera aria from which it borrows its construction) is fundamentally a vocal work or whether it might better be regarded as an instrumental piece in which a voice participates. The vocal line is clearly modeled on the instrumental ritornello; in the "Laudamus te," it even takes on the virtuosity and ornamental character of the string writing. It might be an overstatement to claim that this sort of movement is fundamentally instrumental, but we would never describe old-style movements that way. This is a feature of the modern style. (It is certainly striking when the singer enters after an instrumental ritornello of unified strings; surely our ears are drawn to the human voice and to its presentation of text. But our very tendency to think of voices and instruments as distinct—even opposed—might lead us to think of the voice as central despite the overwhelming domination of instruments in dimensions other than timbre.)

One terminological note: Bach did not call the "Laudamus te" or solo vocal pieces in Mass settings *arias*, even though they are for solo voice and behave very much like an opera or cantata aria. The term aria actually referred to a piece of poetry that served as the text of a vocal movement; the "Laudamus te" and all the other solo movements in the *Mass in B Minor* set the prose text of the Greek and Latin Ordinary of the Mass, not poetry, so Bach did not call them arias.

With the "Confiteor" as an example of old style and the "Laudamus te" representing the modern, we can examine the other movements of the *Mass in B Minor* to see how Bach uses the two styles. To begin, the "Laudamus te" belongs to a group of solo vocal movements that use the modern style. Each is in ritornello form, beginning and ending with the presentation of an instrumental ritornello and articulating vocal segments with partial or complete restatements. This includes the "Qui sedes," the "Et in Spiritum Sanctum," the "Benedictus," and the "Agnus Dei," whose relationship is obvious (audio examples 3.8a–3.8g) 🔊. The "Domine Deus/Domini Fili," a duet discussed in chapter 2, breaks off before the return of its opening material but until that point is characteristic in its construction. The "Quoniam tu solus sanctus" leads directly into the next movement but is fully recognizable. And the "Christe eleison," "Domine Deus," and "Et in unum Dominum" are duets, composed for two voices rather than one but otherwise identical in construction to the aria-like solo pieces.

These movements are all representatives of the modern style and stand in contrast to the "Confiteor" and the "Kyrie eleison II." But you are likely to object that comparing these solo ritornello movements in modern style to choral movements in old style is artificial. The answer is that modern ritornello form and writing also play a role in choral movements in the *Mass in B Minor*—in fact, most of its choral movements are of this type. They are constructed in the same way, based on an instrumental ritornello heard in full or in part throughout the movement, with vocal episodes (often thematically related to the ritornello) heard between statements. You have to listen to these a little differently from the solo ritornello pieces but can clearly hear that their musical language and construction are very similar.

The easiest of these to understand is the "Gloria in excelsis Deo," which begins with a characteristic ritornello (audio example 3.9a) ◉. The typical moment of repose after the ritornello's opening idea is subtle and easy to miss, but the middle spinning-out section and the drive to a cadence (just before the voices enter) are easy to hear. During the course of this movement, the abbreviated return of ritornello material is short indeed but still audible (audio example 3.9b) ◉. The movement leads directly into the "Et in terra pax"—there is no purely instrumental restatement of the opening ritornello—but it does, in fact, have a closing ritornello. At about 1:20 in this short movement, the opening material returns in its original form and in its original key. All the instrumental lines are there, just as at the start of the piece. The difference is that this time, Bach adds the voices, layering their material over the instrumental ritornello (audio example 3.9c) ◉. The final ritornello is thus presented jointly by voice and instruments, a characteristic gesture of choral ritornello movements. The "Qui tollis peccata mundi" and the "Et expecto resurrectionem," each of which is also a ritornello-form movement, do the same thing, presenting a closing ritornello in both voices and instruments rather than in instruments alone as in a typical solo vocal movement. (There are other features of each of these movements that make the structure difficult to hear, but it is there.) Two other choral ritornello movements, the "Et resurrexit" and the "Osanna in excelsis," do have full instrumental ritornellos at the end.

There is one more thing you need to know to be able to hear these movements as modern ritornello pieces that are fundamentally like the solo movements. In the *Mass in B Minor*, choral ritornello movements often omit their opening ritornello; this is true of the "Qui tollis," the "Et resurrexit," and the "Osanna in excelsis," each of which starts with both voices and instruments (audio examples 3.10a–3.10c) ◉. The "Et resurrexit" and the "Et expecto resurrectionem" are ambiguous; one way to hear them is as movements that do have an opening instrumental ritornello but one with voices overlaid on portions of the instrumental material.

Two questions come to mind about the analytical claim that these choruses are ritornello movements without opening ritornellos. One is why Bach would do this, eliminating the most characteristic feature. The answer is probably that he wanted to begin these movements with voices (and thus text) right away, for example, in the "Et resurrexit," where these words immediately follow the text "passus et sepultus est" (audio example 3.11) ◉. (This is discussed at greater length in chapter 2.)

The other question is how a listener might know that these are ritornello movements if they do not have opening ritornellos. This one is tougher to answer. One reason is retrospective: the various partial ritornellos and the full closing ritornello (whether instrumental or vocal-instrumental) confirm the construction after the fact. The other reason is that there are cues from musical syntax, harmony, and the relationship of voice and instruments, elements that are closely tied up with ritornello forms and modern style. In a way, those stylistic markers are more important to the *Mass* overall. These are modern movements; their construction happens to derive from ritornello form, but their status as up-to-date pieces is audible whatever their formal organization.

With an understanding both of old-style contrapuntal movements and of modern, concerted ritornello movements both solo and choral, we are in a position to listen to the other movements in the *Mass in B Minor* from an eighteenth-century perspective and see what Bach has done to reconcile the presence of the two very different styles in this work. In fact, he deploys them carefully and (most interestingly) demonstrates a range of ways in which these styles, fundamentally opposed, can be reconciled. (See table 3.1.)

Perhaps the easiest to hear are his extensions of old style in the direction of the new. The first extension might be the "Kyrie II" itself, which builds an old-style movement on modern chromatic material (using notes outside the movement's key and scale). The "Credo in unum Deum" has all the markers of old style: polyphonic imitation of five independent voices, melodic lines of limited range, a cantus firmus chant intonation by the bass voice toward the end of the movement, a steady walking bass of the kind typical of eighteenth-century adaptations of old style (a modern feature, for sure, but closely linked with the old style), and antiquated notation invisible to the listener but unmistakable on the page. Bach probably turned to this style here in recognition of the liturgical practice of intoning (chanting) the first words of the "Credo in unum Deum" even when the rest of the text is presented in a concerted setting. In this movement, Bach turns to old style for a setting that draws on a chant intonation of the opening Credo text.

He did precisely the same thing in adding a movement to a Mass setting by early-eighteenth-century Bolognese composer Giovanni Battista Bassani. Bassani's work is in modern style, but late in his life, Bach composed a setting (known as BWV 1081) of the words "Credo in unum Deum" in old style to begin the Nicene Creed (audio example 3.12) 🔊. The features are familiar in an eighteenth-century adaptation of old style: a walking bass (here in a repeating melodic pattern), old-fashioned notation, singable melodic lines, and imitation among the voices. (The new "Credo" was necessary because most older musical settings of the Nicene Creed began with its second textual phrase, "Patrem omnipotentem," expecting that the first words would be intoned (sung in unaccompanied chant) by the celebrant, and more elaborate music typically picked up at "Patrem omnipotentem.")

In the "Credo in unum Deum" in the *Mass in B Minor*, Bach also extends the old style. After each of the five voices (tenor, bass, alto, soprano 1, and soprano 2, in that order) has entered in imitation, Bach introduces two more lines (audio example 3.13) 🔊. Those two additional "voices" are violin 1 and violin 2 in the instrumental ensemble. They do not simply double the voices, as one would expect in an old-style movement, but have independent lines as they would in a modern concerted setting. What they play is not characteristically modern. Rather, the violins behave exactly like additional voices in a higher range, producing a seven-part polyphonic texture and deviating only for a small flourish at the end of the movement.

The piece never departs from its old style but finds a role for instruments whose independence from the voices is borrowed from modern concerted music. This is one way Bach reconciles old and new styles: by composing a movement in which instruments from the modern style participate as though they were voices in the old. (This movement turns out to predate the assembly of the *Mass in B Minor*, and it is possible that Bach composed it to use with another Mass setting, just as with his "Credo" intonation for the Bassani Mass.)

This movement represents a small gesture, but two others go even farther in the same direction. The "Gratias agimus tibi" and the "Dona nobis pacem" (which use the same music) extend old style even more. Each of the movements begins in a way that points clearly to old style, from archaic notation to imitative entrances of the voices to simple singable lines to a strictly doubling role of the instruments to the invention of distinct ideas for each textual phrase ("Gratias agimus tibi / propter magnam gloriam tuam") (audio example 3.14a and 3.14b) 🔊.

The first hint of an expansion beyond old style comes about one minute in, when an entrance of the soprano on the text "Gratias agimus tibi" is doubled by trumpet (audio example 3.14c) 🔊. Doubling is, of course, routine in this style, and in fact, the soprano line is already doubled by the first violin and the first oboe in this movement.

But a trumpet doubling is most unusual; trumpets were used for their associations with royalty and military topics, and when deployed in a group of three with kettledrums (as in this work), they were almost exclusively used in movements in modern style, playing characteristic and idiomatic material. Here, though, the first trumpet plays a vocal line and is subservient to the voice it shadows.

Bach does the same thing again a few measures later, accustoming the ear to the very presence of trumpets in an old-style movement. This in itself represents a reconciling of old and new styles, though in a modest way. The real surprise comes at about the two-minute mark, when the first and second trumpet enter in imitation of each other playing the main vocal subject that usually carries the text "Gratias agimus tibi" (audio example 3.14d) ◉. Like the two violins in the "Credo in unum Deum," they become part of the old-style imitative contrapuntal texture. To modern ears, especially those that know the work well, the stylistic mixture here may not stand out, but in eighteenth-century terms, it is striking; trumpets do not usually do this, if ever.

Bach seals the reconciling of old and new styles by what happens next: The third trumpet and the drums enter, and together with the first and second trumpets, they contribute a characteristic brass flourish to make a close; the same kind of writing brings the movement to its glorious conclusion (audio example 3.14e) ◉. The moment is musically compelling in many ways, but perhaps most important is that it marks the complete integration of old and new, with a layering of very modern trumpet writing over old-style vocal polyphony. Bach has taken the reconciliation of old and new a step farther than even in the "Credo in unum Deum" by integrating instruments into old style, here eventually having them playing characteristically modern material. His gradual introduction of this element guides the ear toward what he is doing.

The reconciliation of old and new styles in the *Mass in B Monor* also takes place from the other direction, in modern ritornello-form movements that draw on musical elements associated with the old style. These principally take the form of choral movements using the full instrumental ensemble in which the material presented by the voices is contrapuntal and imitative, referring to the old style. Sometimes these are difficult to spot as ritornello movements, as in the three movements—the "Et in terra pax," the "Cum Sancto Spiritu," and the "Pleni sunt coeli" section of the Sanctus—that begin with voices, dispensing with the opening ritornello that would make their identity clear from the start. In these movements, ritornellos articulate passages of contrapuntal imitation in the voices (alone or doubled by instruments) usually based on material derived from the ritornello. You can get the best sense of this by listening carefully to the way each movement ends, with the full forces playing a final statement of the material; the ritornello quality of these statements is particularly clear (audio examples 3-15a–3-15c) 🎵. And of course, the kind of material sung and played also points to the modern style.

These movements represent a reconciliation of new and old styles only to a degree, it must be admitted. They are modern ritornello forms, which accounts for new style. Their vocal material points in the direction of old-style polyphony but is distinctly more modern. The kind of musical material, the nature of the vocal writing, and the particular contrapuntal treatment owe a great deal to modern (that is, eighteenth-century) fugal writing; if they were stripped of the ritornellos and instrumental participation, you would never mistake the vocal lines for a sixteenth-century work. But the pervasive imitation and the limited instrumental roles in these passages—doubling or very simple chordal accompaniment—point to a vocally conceived texture, just as in the Palestrina style. In this sense, the movements do represent a blending of old and new elements: ritornello forms framing vocal material presented largely as imitative counterpoint.

The most stunning example is the "Kyrie eleison I," which opens the *Mass*. At ten minutes, even at a relatively quick tempo, this might be Bach's longest ritornello-form movement. And a ritornello movement it is, even though most discussions approach it a "choral fugue" or in some way that takes its vocal writing as the focus. In fact, the best way to understand this piece is as an instrumentally structured ritornello work; hearing the piece that way lets you understand how Bach explored the relationship between new and old styles right at the start of the *Mass*. It takes some careful listening to grasp this, but it is worth the effort precisely because Bach's approach in this movement is essential to the stylistic relationships he demonstrates in the work.

The starting point for listening to this piece as a ritornello movement is, unsurprisingly, the opening ritornello itself (audio example 3.16a) 🎵. Lasting the better part of two minutes, it is particularly elaborate and full of musical ideas. Most concerto and aria ritornellos are melodic, with one leading line over an accompanying bass. A few, particularly in Bach's hands, incorporate imitation between two parts. In this ritornello, there are two leading melodic lines played by flute 1-oboe 1 and by flute 2-oboe 2; strings provide an accompaniment. After the slow declamatory opening of the movement (a stereotyped feature of Mass settings, incidentally), the ritornello unfolds contrapuntally, with imitation between the two pairs of woodwind instruments. This is most audible at the start, where they enter with the same musical idea separated by a few measures. This same musical idea enters again at the very end of the ritornello, this time in the bass line, where it signals the approaching cadence. The ritornello of the first movement of Bach's concerto for two violins BWV 1043 works very similarly, with three entrances of a subject at the start and one more to conclude the ritornello (audio example 3.16b) 🔊.

In the "Kyrie eleison I," Bach has designed a modern ritornello in which imitation between two lines plays a large role, and that imitation is the link, of course, to the older musical style. The two large vocal segments of the work unfold with imitation among the five voices, along the lines of imitative old-fashioned counterpoint (though much updated) and using the same musical subject as the ritornello (audio examples 3.16c and 3.16d) 🔊. So both the modern ritornello and the backward-pointing vocal episodes rely on imitation, in different ways, of the same material.

Bach's accomplishment lies in the way he assembles these two presentations into one unified movement. The key is recognizing that the movement has three ritornello statements. The first is the one that opens the movement (after the declamatory opening), presented by instruments alone. The last comes in the last two minutes or so of the movement and is one of those joint vocal-instrumental ritornello statements typical of choral ritornello-form movements. In fact, at the end, the instruments play exactly what they did at the start, but this time, the voices are layered over their ritornello (audio example 3.16e) 🔊.

The second ritornello is identical to the last except that it is heard in a different key; this one is in the middle of the movement and is also presented jointly by voices and instruments (audio example 3.16f) 🔊. So the overall construction is this:

Instrumental ritornello (home key)	Vocal statement	Vocal + instrumental ritornello (different key)	Vocal statement	Vocal + instrumental ritornello (home key)

What makes the movement extraordinary is that the seams between these segments are almost inaudible. That is because Bach joins them in an extremely clever way that is part of his musical point. In the first vocal statement, we hear each of the five voices enter with the subject, just as in many imitative pieces. Then there are two more entrances by soprano 1 and soprano 2, doubled by flutes and oboes. Those entrances sound like Bach's continuation of the imitative exploration of the subject—sixth and seventh vocal entries—but only after the fact do we realize that these two entrances mark the start of a vocal-instrumental ritornello in the middle of the piece. Voices are doubled by flute-oboe pairs—or, maybe better, the flute-oboe pairs of the ritornello's opening are doubled by voices. Those two entrances are simultaneously the sixth and seventh vocal statements of the subject and the imitative start of the ritornello.

He does the same thing a second time toward the end of the movement: vocal imitation (this time in a different order of entry of the voices) merges seamlessly into entrances by soprano 1 and soprano 2 (doubled by flutes and oboes) that turn out also to be the beginning of a ritornello. The very ambiguity is part of Bach's stylistic point, because these soprano-woodwind statements are an expression both of the older-style vocal imitation and of the modern ritornello. Bach's design of an imitative ritornello allowed him to present this musical subject in both guises, and his seamless connection of them audibly demonstrates what they have in common. A ritornello can be constructed with imitation, and a fugal/imitative vocal work can be a ritornello structure. The *Mass in B Minor* doesn't just use the two styles; it has a point to make about their relationship, starting in its very first movement.

And this, I think, is the musical topic of the work. The *Mass in B Minor* presents movements purely in old and new styles but also shows various ways in which they can be reconciled. The old style is represented by movements such as the "Confiteor" and the "Kyrie eleison II," and the possibility of incorporating modern elements (particularly instruments) into the old style is shown in the "Credo in unum Deum" with its voice-like violin parts and by the "Gratias agimus tibi" with its incorporation of trumpets and drums. The modern style is represented by solo ritornello arias and choruses. Several pieces incorporate imitative vocal writing into ritornello forms, especially choral movements and, most strikingly, the "Kyrie eleison I," bringing elements of the vocally based old style into modern movements.

The *B-Minor Mass*'s movements can thus be arrayed on a spectrum with pure old style at one end and pure modern style at the other. Next in from the ends are movements that incorporate elements associated with the other style: instrumental participation in the old-style movements and pervasive vocal counterpoint (admittedly in more modern manifestations) in the new. At the center are the "Gratias agimus tibi" and the musically identical "Dona nobis pacem," with their incorporation of trumpets and drums into an old-style movement.

There are a few other modern movements that are not ritornello forms. The modern imitative "Patrem omnipotentem" presents a fundamentally imitative vocal texture augmented by trumpets and drums, somewhat like the "Gratias agimus tibi" (audio example 3.17) ◎. There are two movements whose basis is the expressive simultaneous declamation of text by the choral voices: the first part of the "Sanctus" (audio example 3.18a) ◎ and the "Et incarnatus est," which probably refers to the motet, an old type of vocal composition, and opens with its characteristic staggered entrances before turning to simultaneous declamation (audio example 3.18b) ◎. The "Crucifixus," whose repeating bass pattern signifies lament, features individual voices for the most part (audio example 3.18c) ◎.

Together with the ritornello movements, these pieces contribute to the numerical domination of movements in the modern style in the *Mass in B Minor*. I think we have to understand this as Bach's starting point; composing a Mass for voices and instruments in the early eighteenth century principally meant writing a concerted work largely in ritornello forms. Old style was special; it was fundamentally even more appropriate to the church than the modern style but was understood as retrospective. A modern composer wrote pieces in the old style as special undertakings, not as a norm, or drew on old style for particular portions of a Mass setting. Unlike the inherently affect-neutral old style, modern style was designed to move the listener. To the extent that this was the goal in Mass composition, eighteenth-century composers drew principally on this evocative way of composing. The *Mass in B Minor* does not attempt to balance old and new styles but rather asks how old style can be meaningfully integrated and reconciled in a modern work.

One of the lasting puzzles of the *Mass in B Minor* is Bach's reuse of the music for the "Gratias agimus tibi" in the work's last movement, the "Dona nobis pacem" (audio example 3.19) ◎. Bach could surely have composed a new movement or reworked another piece rather than duplicate this music. I do not think we can fully explain why he used the same movement, but our stylistic insight can help us understand why the musical style of "Dona nobis pacem" makes a particularly appropriate closing piece. The Mass opens with a ritornello-form movement, the "Kyrie eleison I," in which Bach demonstrates that a contrapuntal ritornello and imitative vocal writing overlap in their compositional technique and that vocal counterpoint can be integrated into a ritornello form. It closes with an old-style movement, the "Dona nobis pacem," that shows how instruments associated with the modern style, trumpets and drums, can be introduced into an old-style piece. The "Dona nobis pacem" is the perfect complement to the "Kyrie eleison I," ending Bach's complete setting of the Mass Ordinary with a reminder of what the work is musically about.

Part II

THE *CHRISTMAS ORATORIO* BWV 248

FOUR

Parody and Its Consequences in the *Christmas Oratorio*

What do we make of the musically secular in a liturgical work?

It has been recognized since the early nineteenth century that Bach's *Christmas Oratorio* consists mostly of parodies, reworkings of arias and choruses he had composed to different texts and for other purposes. (See table 4.1. in the appendix) This is demonstrable, shown both by things you can see in Bach's composing score (where it is evident that he was copying music that had already been written down somewhere else, not inventing it on the page) and in the survival of many of the model compositions that Bach reworked, all definitely older than the *Oratorio*.

But what do we do with this insight? In the case of Bach's *Mass in B Minor*, also mostly the product of parody, the music's origin in older compositions turns out to be of interest mostly for our appreciation of Bach's working methods, not for an understanding of how the piece functions with its new Mass text. The parody origin of most of that work is not audible unless you happen to know the models that for survive for a few of the movements. (This topic is discussed in chapter 2.)

Things are a little different in the *Christmas Oratorio*. As with the *Mass*, there is a lot to be learned from the study of parody about how the piece was put together, which might be of historical or technical interest. But in this work, there are also audible features that point to an origin in older pieces, largely because it is possible to hear that the *Oratorio* relies on compositions of a somewhat different kind from what was usual in Bach's liturgical works. Specifically, there are audible traces of music written for civic rather than religious or liturgical purposes. This raises questions about the relationship between liturgical and secular music in Bach's time and about what it means that Bach could interchange music between the two realms.

One reason the transplantation of the secular models into a liturgical context works so well in the *Christmas Oratorio* is that Bach and his librettist found resonances between the textual and musical topics of the secular works and aspects of the Christmas story. Music that had served a particular purpose in the worldly models was put into similar or at least parallel service in a liturgical context. Some borrowed numbers, on the other hand, would not have worked in their new context and so were transformed in some surprising ways. These pieces point to the particular demands of the Christmas libretto and to Bach and his librettist's desire to make full use of the music of the models they chose to adapt. As with the *Mass* (or any other composition that is the product of parody), this history does not affect the way we listen to the derived work, but the transformations should make us rethink some of our assumptions about the relationship between text and music.

In creating the *Christmas Oratorio* by the parody of existing works, Bach and his librettist evidently aimed, first of all, to use the music of the models they chose as exhaustively as possible. This is easiest to see in the *Oratorio*'s parts I–IV, which they created principally from two works: "Lasst uns sorgen, lasst uns wachen" BWV 213, a piece for the birthday of Electoral Prince Friedrich Christian on September 5, 1733; and "Tönet, ihr Pauken! Erschallet, Trompeten" BWV 214, for the birthday of Electress Maria Josepha on December 8, 1733. Each is a typical work of homage, and each was performed in Leipzig without the presence of the royal honorees; those organizing the performances almost certainly sent copies of the printed texts to Dresden as evidence of their devotion, which was the whole purpose of the works. The December performance took place in Zimmermann's Coffee House, where the Collegium Musicum, a mixed professional and amateur organization, often performed under Bach's direction; the September performance was at the outdoor cafe run by Zimmermann just beyond the city gates during warm weather.

Each was a "dramma per musica," a work with named characters, dialogue, and other features reminiscent of opera. "Tönet, ihr Pauken!" is mostly congratulatory and abstractly allegorical; "Lasst uns sorgen, lasst uns wachen" tells the story of the young Hercules at a moral crossroads and puts the mythological character forward as a virtuous model for the electoral prince. The texts of both cantatas are entirely in verse, consisting of short poems designed to be set as alternating solo arias and recitatives. The Hercules piece also includes two duet arias in which characters interact, one with an "echo" voice.

The outer movements, intended for all the instruments and voices together as framing numbers, also have poetic words and are textually indistinguishable from the solo arias. In fact, they are typically labeled *aria*, just like the solo numbers, and represent so-called tutti arias (arias for all the voices). They were sung by the combined solo voices used in the work (four in total); sometimes they represent the named characters speaking together, and sometimes they depict another group (such as the Council of the Gods and a Chorus of Muses in the Hercules work). These combined four voices formed "the chorus," a label sometimes found on pieces like this but not implying the massed voices we might assume today; such a chorus could be sung by just four singers. The textual and musical character of these tutti arias has significant musical consequences, as we will see.

The construction of these secular works from poetic recitatives and arias (solo, duet, and tutti) formed the starting point for parody because these kinds of movements, particularly the arias, played a significant role in a gospel narrative work such as the *Christmas Oratorio*. An oratorio, in Bach's time, included two textual elements. The first was scriptural narrative set to simple accompaniment (by basso continuo) in a way that resembled the speechlike recitative found in operas and poetic cantatas. Bach almost never called these settings of gospel text *recitative*, a term reserved for settings of poetry. Gospel passages in the *Christmas Oratorio* and Bach's passions (which are oratorios) are labeled "Evang.," meaning either "evangelist" or "gospel."

An oratorio also included a second kind of text: interpretive commentary meant to project a particular theological and affective view of the narrative. This commentary was made up partly of hymn stanzas chosen for their relevance to moments in the scriptural narrative, but most of it consisted of new poetry designed to be set as recitatives and arias reflecting on the gospel words. This is where the borrowed music of the secular cantatas came into the creation of the *Christmas Oratorio*. Secular dramas such as "Tönet, ihr Pauken!" or "Lasst uns sorgen, lasst uns wachen" were the source of the music for poetic movements: solo arias and duets, tutti arias (as opening and possibly closing choruses), and instrumentally accompanied poetic recitatives to the extent that the oratorio libretto called for them and they were adaptable. (This turns out to be trickier than for arias.) Bach newly composed the gospel narrative (mostly the words of an evangelist but also some direct speech of characters and groups) and the hymn settings called for in the libretto; he and his librettist adapted the music and poetry of the borrowed numbers to create the poetic pieces in the oratorio.

We do not know how Bach and his librettist for the *Christmas Oratorio* worked together, but a look at its first four parts gives a good idea of their method. Each of the poetic movements of the two secular cantatas was transformed into a movement in these parts of the *Oratorio*. There are two exceptions: the aria "Blast die wohlgegriffnen Flöten" from one source composition, which they did not use; and "Lust der Völker, Lust der Deinen," the concluding chorus of the other model, which they also skipped. Looked at the other way, they constructed the text of these parts of the *Christmas Oratorio* to use up the arias and choruses from the two model cantatas almost completely. There was one exception, the aria "Schliesse, mein Herze, die selige Wunder," which Bach composed from scratch.

The near-exhaustive use of the models and the design of the *Oratorio* that draws almost all its music from them suggests a working method. It also points to the eighteenth-century understanding of the word *parody*: the construction of a new poem on the model of an existing one. (This is discussed in my preface.) That was precisely the task for the librettist of the *Christmas Oratorio*. Given the texts of the model arias and choruses and plans for their use in the new work (presumably worked out in advance), the librettist needed to write new poems that matched the old in the usual ways—poetic meter, stanza structure, and rhyme scheme—so that the new words could be fitted to the existing music.

The two model cantatas provided opening choruses for the first, third, and fourth parts of the *Oratorio*; they drew, of course, on the models' opening and closing numbers, the ones scored for all the voices and instruments, as was conventional. (See table 4.2.) (The second part does not have an opening chorus.) The one puzzle is the closing chorus of the Hercules cantata, "Lust der Völker, Lust der Deinen," which was not used, and there is a likely explanation. The poetic organization of the text of the opening movement of part V, "Ehre sei dir, Gott, gesungen," matches the text of "Lust der Völker, Lust der Deinen," and it appears that composer and librettist originally planned to use its music to open the fifth part of the *Christmas Oratorio*. Instead, Bach composed a new movement for this spot, apparently changing the plan. This is not certain but would confirm that the original goal was to use the two models as completely as possible.

A look at the music suggests some reasons Bach might have changed his mind and not used "Lust der Völker, Lust der Deinen" to open part V. As the closing movement of the Hercules cantata, "Lust der Völker" matches that work's opening chorus in its use of identical full forces, including two horns. The scoring of an opening number of a large concerted work typically determines the characteristics of its last movement (which almost always matches) as well as parameters of the internal movements. When Bach chose "Lasst uns sorgen, lasst uns wachen," the first movement of the Hercules cantata, to open part IV of the *Christmas Oratorio*, he determined the new work's home key (F major) and instrumentation (strings and horns), just as his use of trumpets and drums in D major at the start of parts I, III, and VI determined the scoring and principal key of those pieces.

For Bach to have started part V of the *Christmas Oratorio* with "Lust der Völker, Lust der Deinen" would have been to force his hand, effectively dictating that this would be a second horn-colored part in a row, in the same key as the preceding one. This might have been a parody that looked good on paper—the new text lines up nicely with the old, as a composer would hope—but the movement was musically not suited to this position in the *Oratorio*. The piece also has a somewhat unusual construction; it is a sort of choral-instrumental dance with solo vocal interludes, an unusual way of putting together a liturgical movement. This, too, might have discouraged Bach from following through on a plan to use it. (The opening movement of the church cantata "Freue dich, erlöste Schar" BWV 30 works very much the same way; more on that piece in a moment.) With the new parody text for the opening of part V written, it made sense for Bach to use it, because it fit into the *Oratorio*'s overall design and set the theological and interpretive tone for this part, but it needed a newly composed setting to distinguish it musically from the previous one.

It is not easy to explain why Bach did not use the music of the aria "Blast die wohlgegriffnen Flöten" in the *Christmas Oratorio*. We could try (and people have), but there is another possibility: perhaps Bach and his librettist did intend to use it somewhere in the first four parts of the *Christmas Oratorio* but later decided to eliminate the aria they had planned. If they made this decision before Bach got to that point in his composing score, we would never know, because our only evidence of the work's genesis is that score. We should not necessarily assume that this movement was rejected. If it wasn't, we are correct in our observation that Bach and his librettist did seek to use all the music of their two models for parts I–IV.

The other gap is the lack of a parody model in either of the two model cantatas for the aria "Schliesse, mein Herze, dies selige Wunder."

It would be an obvious guess that the two exceptions are related, and that Bach and his librettist intended to parody "Blast die wohlgegriffnen Flöten," the one model aria he did not use, to create this one. But the two texts are so different in their construction (starting with their poetic meters) that this seems unlikely. There are possible explanations involving multiple changes of plans and reshuffling of extant music and new *Christmas Oratorio* texts, but none is verifiable. In the end, we know that Bach composed a new aria for this spot in the *Oratorio*, the only freshly written solo aria in the entire work.

The complex history of this movement is instructive, because it shows the benefits of Bach's turning to parody when he could. Bach presumably had a parody planned but decided to start from scratch instead. In the autograph score, he began composing a new aria for this text, but gave up and crossed out his draft after a few measures. Then he started over with a very different sort of movement, the one we know today—effectively his third try. Bach was a facile composer, but it is striking to see him think and rethink this one new movement; it is as if the parody process, stimulated by his librettist, engaged a different part of his creative abilities and he had to restart his compositional engine.

Bach and his librettist derived parts I–IV from two model compositions they evidently aimed to reuse completely. Parts V and VI at first appear to have been created in a different way, but the process turns out to be very similar. We can be sure that the music of the poetic movements of these parts derived from older works, aside from the opening chorus of part V which was newly composed after Bach apparently abandoned a parody plan for it. We know this in the usual ways for most of the movements, including evidence from the autograph score that shows Bach was copying and revising rather than composing on the page. But we also know that the poetic movements of part VI were parodies because we have evidence of their lost model—not directly, as with the two surviving models for parts I–IV, but in a somewhat more roundabout way.

The evidence is an incomplete set of original performing parts that document a Bach church cantata sharing almost all the movements of part VI of the *Christmas Oratorio*. We do not know the text of that church cantata or its liturgical purpose (only untexted instrumental parts survive, and none identifies the occasion for the work). But the presence of a chorale setting at the end confirms that it was indeed a liturgical piece. The performing parts for this cantata turn up in an interesting place: among the original performing materials for part VI of the *Christmas Oratorio* itself.

This takes a little explaining. The performing parts for all the other parts of the *Christmas Oratorio* were copied from scratch; the autograph score was handed to a team of copyists, and they produced the parts starting with blank pieces of paper. To create the material for part VI, though, Bach began by recycling some parts that already contained almost all the music he wanted to use.

Those were the parts for that lost church cantata; he simply doctored them so they could be the basis of the performing material for part VI of the *Oratorio*. This was a time-saving device Bach occasionally used in making parodies. If a derived work used most or all of the music of an older one, adding few or no movements, and if its adaptation consisted mostly of new vocal lines, keeping the instrumental lines intact, all that was required was to make new vocal parts with the new words and notes adjusted to fit them. Instrumental parts could be reused, any unparodied movements could just be crossed out, and any new movements (such as the hymn settings typical of church cantatas) could be added. This saved the considerable labor (and paper) of copying out new instrumental parts.

That is exactly what happened in part VI of the *Christmas Oratorio*. Bach reused three instrumental parts from the church cantata, which contained almost all of the nongospel movements in part VI. The retained material consisted of parts for violin 1, violin 2, and basso continuo—all instrumental parts, as in other parodied Bach works. The only addition necessary in the violin parts was a new chorale harmonization, and it was a simple matter to insert it at the bottom of a page or at the end of a part, as it is short and musically simple. The continuo part also needed the gospel narrative added, and of course, Bach and his assistants created new parts for voices (with the new texts) and for other instruments.

This procedure—adapting a church cantata wholesale—looks like a somewhat different procedure from the one Bach used in creating the earlier parts of the *Christmas Oratorio*—note that the source composition was a church cantata, not a secular work. But there is more going on here. Various features of the borrowed movements and their sources point to an even earlier history of this music, dating from before the church cantata whose parts were reused. That is, the origin of the parodied movements in part VI (and probably also much of part V) was not ultimately that church cantata but another piece that lay, in turn, behind it.

You can hear the first hints in the opening chorus of part VI, "Herr, wenn die stolzen Feinde schnauben" (audio example 4.1) 🔊. Its textual and musical ABA organization is that of a typical aria; each of its vocal sections begins with entrances of the voices one by one but moves toward a four-voice texture in which all the parts move together and in which you can clearly hear the poetic meter of the text. Those are the features of the kind of chorus that typically opens a secular cantata, leading to the strong suspicion that this music was composed not for the church cantata but for some secular purpose.

Among the movements in part VI that were created by parody are not only a poetic chorus and arias but also instrumentally accompanied recitatives. Parodied movements of this kind tend to appear in Bach's church works adapted from a secular cantata, a kind of piece in which instrumentally accompanied recitative often plays a large role. The next-to-last movement of the *Christmas Oratorio*, for example, is a recitative joined by all four voices, the kind one finds near the end of a secular cantata as an introduction to the final tutti aria. There are two poetic solo recitatives in part VI and one in part V, which might make us wonder about the origin of their music, too. The dancelike construction of the aria "Nur ein Wink von seinen Händen," both in the nature of its musical material and in its organization, is of a sort one expects in a secular cantata rather than in an original liturgical one (audio example 4.2) ◉.

And the very construction of the model church cantata (to the extent we can reconstruct it) consisting entirely of movements on poetic texts, apparently starting with a tutti aria and alternating arias and recitatives (except for a concluding chorale), is found only in Bach's church cantatas derived by the movement-by-movement retexting of a secular work.

The church cantata "Freue dich, erlöste Schar" BWV 30 is a good example of this kind. (audio example 4.3a) ◉. The model is a secular cantata, "Angenehmes Wiederau" BWV 30a, which Bach had composed for a member of the nobility, a musical drama with named allegorical characters (Fate, Good Fortune, Time, and the river Elster) (audio example 4.3b) ◉. The work consists of an opening tutti aria, musically repeated at the end with a somewhat different text; a series of recitative-aria pairs for the various characters; and a four-voice recitative just before the final tutti aria. The church cantata derived from it takes over the framing choruses and almost all the arias, fitted with new texts. One recitative-aria pair in the middle is replaced with a chorale setting that divides the new liturgical work in two, and the recitatives are newly composed. To perform the work, Bach doctored the instrumental parts from the secular cantata as necessary and made new ones for the four voices and for organ.

The cantata "Erhöhtes Fleisch und Blut" BWV 173 (audio example 4.3c) 🔊, derived from a secular work from Cöthen, "Durchlauchster Leopold" BWV 173a (audio example 4.3d) 🔊, works similarly. Bach simply dropped one aria and a recitative to make a shorter church work with a new liturgical text. In this cantata, he even retained the music of the recitatives, entering the new text under the older secular one in his composing score. We don't have the performing parts for this work, but it is a good bet that Bach reused the instrumental material.

Church cantatas created in this way from a secular work have characteristic musical features, and the piece that probably lies behind part VI of the *Christmas Oratorio* shows them. Its music likely comes ultimately from a secular cantata, just as the music of parts I–IV does. The terzet aria in part V, which we know is also a parody, could well come from this same source.

And now the derivation of parts V and VI of the *Christmas Oratorio* looks a lot more like that of parts I–IV. Bach appears to have reused the music of a secular model to create the final two parts of the *Oratorio*, deriving it from the same work from which he created the lost church cantata. The only movement that definitely came from another source is the aria "Erleucht auch meine finstre Sinnen" in part V. Bach parodied this from yet another cantata for the Saxon royal house, using just one movement rather than an entire piece. This might well have been a last-minute measure after some aspect of an original plan changed, but it might also have represented part of the original plan if composer and librettist needed one more aria than their models offered. The strategy is clear and even suggests more about a working method: Bach probably pointed his librettist to the texts of the three large secular cantatas, from which the poet produced new texts and (probably together with Bach) a plan for the six parts of the oratorio.

It is worth mentioning that we do not know the identity of the *Christmas Oratorio*'s librettist. The text of one of the two model cantatas we have been examining, the Hercules piece, is by Christian Friedrich Henrici, an amateur poet who used the pen name Picander and who also wrote the librettos for Bach's *St. Matthew Passion* and the lost *St. Mark Passion*, among other works. We know it is his because he reprinted the libretto in one of the collections of his occasional poetry he issued periodically. But the text of the other model for the first four parts is anonymous; it is probably not by Picander, because he did not reprint it. And we have no idea about lost work that apparently lies behind parts V and VI.

We would certainly like to know who wrote the *Christmas Oratorio* parody texts, and it has been speculated that Picander was responsible for them. In fact, we know he was skilled at making this kind of adaptation, but he is not credited in the printed libretto of the work available for sale to churchgoers, nor does the text appear in any of those collections of his poetry. We simply do not know who the *Christmas Oratorio*'s librettist was, and stylistic guesses are of limited value; some of the *Oratorio*'s texts arguably sound like Picander's poetry, but some are adaptations of his writings, after all, and might resemble his work because of that derivation, not because he wrote them.

The matter is significant because it has been repeatedly suggested that Bach and his librettist planned the *Christmas Oratorio* at the time they were creating the secular cantatas whose music they reused in it. This theory is unlikely for several reasons, at least in its simplest form. Until all the source compositions existed, it would have been difficult to plan an entire oratorio, and I do not think Bach necessarily knew in advance which occasions would present the opportunity of composing a new secular work that could later serve as the source of movements for a planned oratorio. The authorship of the texts matters to this question because the *Christmas Oratorio* was not Bach's creation alone; it was undertaken together with a poet. If the work was mapped out in advance, its planning likely would have been done by both Bach and a librettist. But more than one person was probably responsible for the texts of the secular cantatas that were reused, making it difficult to see how the planning would have worked.

The suggestion that Bach planned the *Christmas Oratorio* even as he was composing the secular works may have an ideological element. Since the work's revival in the middle of the nineteenth century, there has been some degree of queasiness over Bach's use of secular musical sources for the *Oratorio*. I suspect that some of this worry lingers, even among those who have abandoned any sense of impropriety in Bach's liturgical use of music originally in honor of elector and king and featuring mythological and political topics. It might be easier to accept that Bach used these secular models for a liturgical purpose if we believe that he planned all along to make liturgical works from the material. In fact, this was precisely the strategy used by the first commentators on the *Christmas Oratorio* in the nineteenth century (discussed in chapter 6), who used it to wriggle out of their discomfort with the *Oratorio*'s origin in secular works. It would not surprise me if, in general, Bach did have it in mind to reuse the music of large-scale civic works even as he composed and performed them, reflecting an understandable desire to find more than one day's use for compositions. But I do not think we have to postulate that he planned the *Christmas Oratorio* all along; maybe he did, but we should probably insist on some evidence, of which there appears to be none.

Bach had a lot of occasional music to draw on, because there is a large repertory, both in surviving pieces and in works whose existence is known from texts or other evidence but whose music is lost. These include works for rulers (elector, king, prince, duke, and their family members) on various occasions (birthdays, name days, coronations, anniversaries of ascent, New Year's festivities, weddings); for members of the nobility, university professors, and St. Thomas School officials; for university events, particularly in honor of rulers (a memorial service, birthdays); for the St. Thomas School (commemorating a new building, installing a new rector); for weddings; and for miscellaneous performances by the Collegium Musicum. Bach composed some of these works in the course of his duties, for example, at the court in Cöthen, where he served as *Capellmeister*, or in his position in the St. Thomas School. Some he wrote on commission as a guest of courts; others represented paid work, particularly those for the large public events in Leipzig that honored the Saxon elector and his family. Still others grew out of Bach's direction of the Collegium Musicum.

Bach studies have not known quite what to do with this diverse collection. The generic label *secular cantata* hardly seems appropriate, because the category includes everything from a chamber piece such as the *Coffee Cantata* BWV 211, meant for performance (appropriately enough) in a Leipzig coffee house, to the spectacular double-chorus work with trumpets and drums "Preise dein Glücke, gesegnetes Sachsen" BWV 215, performed outdoors for a visit of the Saxon elector.

Bach's "secular cantatas" (or maybe better called nonliturgical cantatas) certainly have features that distinguish them from the church works, including their tendency toward drama, their inclusion of named characters who speak, and their mythological and allegorical subjects. But the secular works and the liturgical ones share a great deal, because they are all ultimately derived from the same source: opera. The secular cantatas alternate poems meant to be set as declamatory recitatives with affective arias, which is also the basic construction of opera. The dramatic cantatas particularly resemble opera in this regard, with a careful distribution of arias among their characters, just as in an opera. A characteristic feature of Bach's secular cantatas is their choral movements, usually opening and closing a work with full forces; these have parallels in opera but are nowhere near as prominent.

Church cantatas of the kind Bach composed after c. 1711 bear a close resemblance to these secular works in many ways. Modern church cantatas retained the use of hymns and scriptural texts, a feature inherited from church music of the seventeenth century, but added a new element: free poetry designed to be set as recitatives and arias. The pioneer of this kind of libretto, theologian and poet Erdmann Neumeister, likened the new kind of church cantata to an excerpt from an opera, and in fact, this is the origin of the modern term *cantata* used to refer to these pieces. Bach mostly called his church pieces *concerto*, reserving cantata for the works that most resembled opera in consisting entirely or mostly of poetic texts and focusing on solo vocal writing.

The poetic and musical origins of secular and liturgical cantatas were thus the same, by way of opera, so it is no surprise that they share so many features. The closest resemblance lies in the internal movements, which, in both church and secular cantatas, often consist mostly of solo recitatives and arias. Church cantata librettos are typically not purely poetic, though, except for a few pieces consisting entirely of poetic recitatives and arias for a solo voice; they usually include scriptural passages (particularly prominent as opening movements) and chorale stanzas (very often closing a work). Secular cantatas, on the other hand, typically open and close with tutti arias sung by all the voices. Like the secular works, church cantatas also typically begin and end by convention with movements that use all the forces, but they are usually not poetic arias.

There is a small group of exceptions in Bach's output: church cantatas derived from secular works. When Bach chose to adapt all or most of the movements of a secular cantata, the process brought the musical features of the secular work with it, including an opening (and sometimes closing) poetic chorus. ("Freue dich, erlöste Schar" BWV 30, discussed earlier, is an example.) Bach did not tend to compose original church works in this way; nothing prevented him from doing so, but most of the librettos he was provided with, certainly by the time he worked in Leipzig, do not open with a free poetic chorus.

A big exception is his Passion settings. In keeping with their emphasis on the affective telling and interpretation of the Passion story, each opens with a poetic chorus: "Herr, unser Herrscher" in the first version of the *St. John Passion*, the dialogue "Kommt, ihr Töchter" at the start of the *St. Matthew Passion*, and "Geh, Jesu, geh zu deiner Pein," which opened the lost *St. Mark Passion*. Those works end (or nearly do) with poetic movements as well, the first version of the *St. John Passion* and the *St. Matthew Passion* with stylized poetic lullabies (followed by a chorale in most versions of the *St. John*) and an ensemble aria about Jesus's burial in the *St. Mark Passion*.

But most church cantatas do not open with new poetry; one by Bach that begins with a choral aria is likely an adaptation of a secular work, and there are usually perceptible traces of that origin. The opening movements of these works make the poetic meter of their text audible, and they use the voices as a unified ensemble, at least for much of the movement, declaiming the text together, as in the opening of "Freue dich, erlöste Schar."

The parts of the *Christmas Oratorio* fall into this category of church pieces with poetic openings (audio examples 4.4a–4.4e) ⓢ. Part I opens with the chorus "Jauchzet, frohlocket," in which the voices declaim the text together; the opening chorus of part III, "Herrscher des Himmels, erhöre das Lallen," begins with individual vocal entrances but quickly moves to simultaneous delivery of the poetry; "Fallt mit Danken, fallt mit Loben," at the start of part IV, uses the voices almost exclusively as a unit; in part VI, the voices once again begin independently but move inexorably toward simultaneous presentation of the text. The opening chorus of part V, "Ehre sei dir, Gott, gesungen," is particularly telling. Bach composed this anew, as we have seen, probably abandoning an original plan to use the last movement of the Hercules cantata. Presented with a poetic opening text, he composed a movement that emphasizes the voices' unity—a choral aria—responding to the prosody of the text. Part II opens, of course, with an instrumental movement that captures the pastoral topic of the second day's narrative, combining two musical stereotypes of the pastoral familiar in the eighteenth century: a gently lilting dance played by strings and a stylized imitation of rustic bagpipes played by the oboe choir (audio example 4.4f) ⓢ.

The consistent use of poetic opening movements contributes to the *Christmas Oratorio*'s character. Scriptural text is restricted to gospel narrative of the story; it does not provide the texts of opening movements, as in many church cantatas. Chorale stanzas are likewise used as moments of reflection within each part and as ending movements; they do not supply opening movements as in Bach's cycle of cantatas based on chorales. The musical prominence of the *Oratorio*'s poetic opening movements, their tendency toward dance rhythms (every one is in a triple meter, strongly associated with dance), and their uniformly major keys lend the parts of the *Christmas Oratorio* a distinctive tone. The affinity with secular cantatas is unmistakable and depends on the subtle but important ways in which Bach's liturgical and secular cantatas differed. The movements are not so much transformed as transplanted, along with their festive and celebratory tone, into the liturgical work. Unlike most other elements that stem from parody, this is audible in the derived composition.

The successful adaptation of the solo arias by Bach and his librettist worked a little differently and depended largely on resonances between the original secular contexts and the new liturgical one. These typically involved conventions of solo arias that were familiar from opera but found new meaning in a work such as the *Christmas Oratorio*. A good example is the aria "Schlafe, mein Liebster," whose musical features would have been instantly recognizable to eighteenth-century listeners (audio example 4.5a) 🔊. They would have heard the static harmony of the opening ritornello (the entire opening is presented over a sustained note in the bass register), the sweet sound of two upper melodic lines moving together, and the many groupings of notes in pairs.

These features, replicated in the vocal sections, heard together were musical emblems of sleep. Sleep scenes were common in contemporary opera, especially French works of the late seventeenth century and pieces that took them as models. The classic example of the type, known as a *sommeil*, is from the third act of Jean-Baptiste Lully's *Atys* (1689), an extended scene in which the title character is given a message of love in a dream. The opening instrumental sinfonia is characteristic, with notes grouped in twos and sustained pitches creating static harmony (audio example 4.5b) 🔊.

There is an exact parallel in Handel's mythological near-opera *Semele* from 1744. A scene for Somnus, the god of sleep, opens the third act, and its music—harmonically static and featuring paired notes—closely echoes Lully's *sommeil* (audio example 4.5c) 🔊. In fact, this was a stereotype by the early eighteenth century and found an expression in vocal numbers as well. Handel's aria for Somnus in the same scene, "Leave me, loathsome light," has many of the same features (audio example 4.5d) 🔊. The type also appears in Bach's church cantatas; most famous is the aria "Schlummert ein, ihr matten Augen" from the cantata "Ich habe genung" BWV 82, where the sleep invoked is death (audio example 4.5e) 🔊.

The *Christmas Oratorio*'s "Schlafe, mein Liebster" is of exactly this type, and there is little surprise in finding that its parody model is a sleep aria from the Hercules cantata whose text also begins "Schlafe, mein Liebster" (Sleep, my most beloved) (audio example 4.5f) 🔊. The context is a little different. Bach and Picander's drama narrates Hercules's moral choice between virtue and vice—more precisely between Virtue and Vice, who are personified as allegorical characters. "Schlafe, mein Liebster" is Vice's aria of seduction in which Hercules is invited to sleep to taste passion. Of course, the *Christmas Oratorio* version steers clear of this language; sleep is summoned as a refreshing pleasure rather than something erotic. The preceding recitative explicitly introduces the aria as a lullaby, a performed piece, not just commentary in an abstract voice.

And this is where the resonance lies, because cradle songs for the infant Jesus had long been a part of musical treatments of the nativity story. Three of the little concertos ("intermedii") in Heinrich Schütz's *Christmas Historia*, for example, are based on a rocking motive that the composer explicitly connects with the rocking of Jesus's cradle (audio example 4.5g) ◉. "Schlafe, mein Liebster" is at home in Bach's *Christmas Oratorio* because composer and librettist found a connection between an operatic sleep piece and the tradition of cradle songs in treatments of the Christmas story. Parody here represents more than a reuse of notes; the liturgical and secular worlds overlap.

There are other parallels and resonances like this between Bach's models and the movements of the *Christmas Oratorio*. The aria "Flösst, mein Heiland, flösst dein Namen" (audio example 4.6a) ◉ shares music with an aria from the Hercules cantata in which the hero explicitly addresses Echo for advice on his moral dilemma and is answered (audio example 4.6b) ◉. It turns out that there was a well-established tradition of sacred echo dialogues, in which it was understood that responses represent the words of Jesus, and this made an ideal model for an aria in the *Oratorio*.

In the aria "Grosser Herr, o starker König" in the *Oratorio*'s first part, the use of a trumpet acknowledges the text's identification of Jesus as "great Lord and King"—a striking statement about a newborn, with significant theological meaning (audio example 4.7a) ◉. But it is also ironic as a reflection of the worldly splendor ("Pracht," a word that appears twice in the short poem) that the text explicitly says Jesus disdains. The secular model is an aria in praise of the Saxon electress and queen (audio example 4.7b) ◉. It addresses her by title ("Königin"), but the trumpet does not primarily signify her royalty, as it often does. Instead, it is connected to the character who sings the aria, a bass who represents Fama (Fame). This figure, Pheme to the Greeks, sometimes carried dark associations with gossip and rumor but in this context spreads the queen's good name around the world. Fama (usually regarded as female but sung by a bass in the cantata) is typically depicted with wings, usually standing on a globe, and always holding a trumpet. The trumpet that sounds in the queen's aria is Fama's.

In the *Christmas Oratorio*, the instrument is made to align with its royal meanings as the aria is transformed. It is possible, of course, that the trumpet could also signify the spreading of the news of Jesus's birth. This is a central concept in the faith, starting with the idea of *gospel* itself—literally good news to be spread. It figures in the opening chorus of the *Christmas Oratorio* ("vaunt what the Highest has done today"); it is in the angel's words to the shepherds quoted in part II ("Behold, I bring you tidings of great joy"); it is part of Martin Luther's Christmas hymn "Vom Himmel hoch, da komm ich her" (From heaven above I come down) used in the *Oratorio*, whose first stanza continues, "Ich bring euch gute neue Mär" (I bring you good news). The spreading of the news of Jesus's birth, as if by Fama, would make interpretive sense as a link between the *Oratorio* text and the musical features of the model.

The problem is that there would be no way for a listener to know that Fama was being invoked by the trumpet unless that were a strong convention, which it does not appear to have been, at least compared with the royal associations of the instrument. The meaning is evident only through the explicit language of the secular cantata, and the alignment might have been privately reserved for Bach and his librettist. This is another bit of inaudible parody; it's valuable instead as an example of the sort of resonance composer and librettist found between their texts.

The cantata from which this aria and much of the *Christmas Oratorio*'s parts I–IV derive is an odd drama in which three female mythological deities praise the queen. One is a goddess of peace (Pax Irene), but the others are goddesses of war (Bellona and Pallas Athena [Minerva]). Fama, who sings the trumpet aria, is the fourth character making up a vocal quartet. The aria sung by Bellona in the cantata calls for flutes to be played and invokes their weaponlike sound; the vocal line begins with a series of repetitions of one pitch that might be meant to invoke trumpet calls, and the bass line under the first vocal entrance is also trumpetlike (audio example 4.8a) ●. Bach draws on this association in another cantata in honor of the Saxon elector and king, with the aria "Durch die von Eifer entflammeten Waffen" from "Preise dein Glücke, gesegnetes Sachsen" BWV 215, in which flutes play military flourishes among their figures (audio example 4.8b) ●.

Modern associations with the flute are benign, and some in the eighteenth century were gentle (for example, in pastoral music), but the instruments were strongly gendered male then and were particularly associated with military officers. Bellona's flute aria from the queen's cantata is "Blast die wohlgegriffnen Flöten," precisely the piece whose music was uniquely not parodied in the *Christmas Oratorio* among the arias in its cantata. One wonders whether it was too militaristic to find a place in the Christmas work, even transformed with a new text, and whether Bach and his librettist deliberately passed over it for this reason. Before we get too comfortable with that explanation, we should note that the one aria Bach did borrow for the *Christmas Oratorio* from outside his main sources was, in fact, "Durch die von Eifer entflammeten Waffen," that other militaristic flute aria for the king. That aria was transformed, though, becoming a piece for oboe d'amore in a new key, "Erleucht auch meinen finstren Sinnen" (audio example 4.8c) ◐. Bach eliminated the flute and with it the instrument's associations.

That aria also underwent another transformation. The model in the secular cantata belongs to a small group of Bach's arias with no role for basso continuo, otherwise present in each movement of every early-eighteenth-century work. The supporting harmonic function usually supplied by continuo is provided in the aria by unison violins and violas, which, of course, play much higher than a usual continuo part in the bass register. There is a handful of such arias without bass in Bach's music; the most famous is probably the soprano aria "Aus Liebe will mein Heiland sterben" from the *St. Matthew Passion* (audio example 4.8d) ◐.

There has been a lot of debate over what it means for Bach to write this special sort of piece. In sacred works, there are certainly theological meanings, although I am not convinced that there is a single unifying significance, as has been argued. In the cantata for the king, the use of this technique, called *bassetto* (little bass) was at least partly practical, not text-expressive; it made its lone soprano and pair of flutes audible in the work's open-air performance outside the king's lodgings in the main Leipzig square.

In the *Christmas Oratorio*, with flutes replaced by oboe d'amore and soprano voice replaced by bass, there was no need to retain the bassless scoring; in fact, that would have been impossible with a bass singer. (All such pieces are for upper voices, as you would probably have guessed.) Bach thus eliminated the aria's two most characteristic features: flute scoring (with military associations) and lack of basso continuo (although he did perform the movement without cello or violone [double bass], with the continuo line played only by organ). This is a good example of the kind of transformation through which Bach could put borrowed material; the aria fit its new context only after he thoroughly reworked it. Bach apparently did believe that listeners would hear the topical significance of a borrowed musical setting in its new context, and he made changes to sidestep that. Without the model, we would have no idea; I challenge anyone to listen to the bass aria "Erleucht auch meinen finstren Sinnen" and conclude that it had originally been a bassless aria for soprano with flutes, in a different key.

Sometimes the musical features of a borrowed movement are simply difficult to understand in relation to the new context. A good example is the duet aria "Herr, dein Mitleid," a text of praise for God's compassion and mercy (audio example 4.9a) 🔊. It uses two voices but is not a dialogue; there is no obvious feature of the text's construction that suggests a duet setting rather than a solo aria. This is often true in original works as well, not just parodies like this one; sometimes the motivation to write a duet rather than a solo aria appears to have been musical, for variety in scoring.

This is more than just an aria sung by two voices, though. The musical construction of the movement is unmistakable to an eighteenth-century ear, with its ritornello played by two harmonizing instruments, matched by the sweetly complementary entrances of the two voices that then proceed tightly together, intertwining intimately. This is a love duet, and no informed listener would have missed the characteristic features. This made perfect sense in the original secular context, where this music is the duet for Hercules and Virtue (his choice, naturally, over Vice) expressed in amorous terms: "I am yours / You are mine / Kiss me / I kiss you" (audio example 4.9b) 🔊.

But why use this music for "Herr, dein Mitleid"? The answer is not at all clear. In the *Christmas Oratorio*, the duet is the third of three movements of commentary after a gospel passage that narrates the shepherds' reaction to the news of Jesus's birth announced by an angel. The first, a recitative, speaks of God comforting and redeeming God's people; the following chorale attributes the event to God's love; and the duet text speaks of God's mercy, compassion, and comforting and of love. The musical markers of a love duet might be meant to compare the believer's relationship with God to the ties between lovers; there is plenty of such imagery in Lutheran thought. This was probably the motivation for Bach's use of another duet of this kind for the "Et in unum Dominum" of the *Mass in B Minor*, where the duet stands for the unity of members of the trinity (audio example 4.9c) 🔊.

The parallel is very close indeed; the score of the Hercules cantata shows that Bach originally planned to use the music we know from the "Et in unum Dominum" for the mythological drama's love duet, then changed his mind and composed the piece we are discussing. (Of course, that makes the "Et in unum Dominum" a love duet, too; this is discussed in chapter 2.)

The use of an amorous duet could represent a reading of the text, and the insertion of this sentiment at this moment in the *Christmas Oratorio* could be an act of interpretation. But there are two things to be cautious about here. First, the context of this movement in part III of the *Oratorio* does not make this an obvious interpretation; although there are some suggestive words in the new duet text, it does not appear to be designed to take much advantage of the musical features of the model even though it takes up its textual topic.

Second, our interpretation of the possible religious significance of the love duet is essentially ad hoc. One runs across this kind of thing all the time in writing on Bach, theological explanations of musical features that assume an obvious and universal meaning of religious texts. For an explanation like this to be convincing, we would want to see it grounded in a thorough historical understanding of eighteenth-century Lutheran theology, not just asserted as though the interpretation of Christian scripture and doctrine were unchanging across time, place, and confession.

In fact, there are sources on eighteenth-century Lutheran theology that support such a reading—that relate divine love and mercy—and at least one other composition by Bach that arguably combines the concept of mercy with music associated with amorous love (the duet "Et misericordia" of Bach's *Magnificat* BWV 243). There is thus a historical argument to be made that the relationship between *Oratorio* text and borrowed music is significant. To put it bluntly, my "explanation" is made up but does not have to be; this is the difference between historically informed theological musical scholarship and ungrounded assertion.

There is little question that the musical type might have been intended to suggest amorous love as a parallel to the sentiments in the duet text. But from a practical point of view, it is also possible that this reuse of the duet might first have been the byproduct of Bach and his librettist's desire to use all the movements of the model cantatas, including this love duet, and that this is simply where this music could be made to fit least awkwardly. It is possible to overinterpret—or at least to attribute more intent to the creators than is warranted. Of course, intent and meaning are related in a complex way, so it is also possible that both these interpretations are correct. Bach's first motivation might have been practical, to use up all the movements of the

Hercules cantata, but the language the librettist chose and the music Bach adapted might still generate these meanings. As we have seen in chapter 2, neither the work's genesis nor the creators' intent determines what the duet meant or means. Even if there is evidence that the initial impulse was practical and connected to the work's assembly, that's all but irrelevant to the piece's meaning.

Occasionally, a movement is transformed in the process of parody. The most famous example in the *Christmas Oratorio* is the work's first aria, "Bereite dich, Zion" (Prepare yourself, Zion), which is part of the first day's interpretive focus on the reception of Jesus's birth (audio example 4.10a) ◐. With its language of "tender desire," its description of Jesus as "most beautiful" and "most beloved," and its invocation of the bridegroom (echoing the poetry of the Song of Songs), the aria's gentle and loving sentiments are evident. They are reflected in features of the music: its graceful triple meter, its leaning figures on so many strong beats (an emblem of longing in eighteenth-century music), its delicate ornamentation with trills and additional short graces, and its isolation and emphasis of the words "den Schönsten" (the most beautiful) and "den Liebsten" (the most beloved). This is an aria of love, and the affect is ardent.

Its parody model from the Hercules cantata never fails to amaze (audio example 4.10b) ◐. That movement comes after Virtue has made a successful case to the young hero; in the aria, Hercules angrily rejects Vice. The vehemence of its text is unmistakable, with its its parallel statements "I will not listen to you / I do not wish to know you," its threefold use of the word "nicht" within just the first two lines, and its reference to the attempt by Hera, the jealous wife of Hercules's father Zeus, to kill the boy in his cradle by means of poisonous serpents. These are all markers of a classic operatic rage aria, right down to the snakes.

Bach's musical setting follows suit. Its violins all play together, in unison, often a marker of a particularly vehement ritornello and aria; a more typical Bach string scoring would provide individual harmonizing lines for two violins and viola. It is marked "staccato," which in eighteenth-century terms called for incisive and even percussive attacks. There are passages of ceaseless short notes, emblems of agitation, in the violins and later in the basso continuo. The vocal line almost obsessively repeats "Ich will nicht . . ." (I will not . . .), is full of awkward and angular vocal phrases, and makes a rhythmically and metrically off-balance cadence on the striking words "zermalmet, zerrissen" (crush, tear apart) at the end of middle section. This is an aria of rejection and rage.

You can hear parallels in music for the character Sesto in Handel's opera *Giulio Cesare in Egitto*. The first part of "Svegliatevi nel core," a classic revenge aria (with a slow middle section for contrast), features unison violin writing at the opening, frequent doubling of the voice by violins for emphasis, and a text that explicitly mentions revenge (audio example 4.10c) 🔊. A later aria for Sesto, "L'angue offeso mai riposa," is somewhat different in musical character, but its text is characteristically about snakes and their venom. Handel also composed English-language pieces of this kind, including the bass solo "Why do the nations rage so furiously together?" from *Messiah*, which draws on many of the same musical devices and particularly emphasizes elaborate vocal writing (audio example 4.10d) 🔊.

Bach's only significant recomposition in changing the rage aria for Hercules into a *Christmas Oratorio* movement is the rewriting of some of the vocal line in the middle section (the part that originally talked about serpents). But most of the broad musical features remain the same: notes of the instrumental lines, key, meter, formal organization, and so on. The transformation took place in details; for example, Bach changed the scoring, doubling the violin line with oboe. The most consequential alterations were in articulation—indications of how to play, separate, and connect notes. The "staccato" indication is gone, and Bach added more phrasing marks to iron out the intentional jaggedness of the original instrumental and vocal lines. This is what produces the graceful character of the *Christmas Oratorio* aria, whose affect—its human emotional tone—is completely transformed.

There are several lessons here. The first is that this is a cautionary example for anybody who believes it is possible to reconstruct Bach's parody process with certainty when the model or the derived composition is lost. The two texts of these arias match in poetic organization but have almost nothing in common, unless you count the almost comical rhyme between "Schlangen" (serpents) in the Hercules text and "Wangen" (cheeks, the infant Jesus's) in the Christmas work or the fact that both the mythological and liturgical texts refer to infants in a cradles. Once again, I do not think anybody, even the boldest speculative reconstructor of lost Bach works, would have the courage to suggest that these two texts belonged to the same music if we did not know.

The second lesson is that sometimes the affective character of an aria, arguably its most important feature and certainly its main musical contribution to a church text, is surprisingly mutable. It is the product of several features of a composition, including instrumentation, articulation, and elements such as tempo that are only implied in eighteenth-century notation. (Almost all performances of the rage aria today are much faster than those of the Christmas piece; this is a matter of interpretation, as there is no way to know how fast these pieces should go, but it makes sense to modern ears, at least.) There are few examples like this in Bach's parody repertory, although, of course, there might be more lurking in parodies for which we lack either the model or the reworked piece. Most parodies carry their affective character from model to derived work, just as they bring other features, but in this example from the *Christmas Oratorio*, the character of the original is contradicted.

What might have prompted Bach and his librettist to use the music of Hercules's rage aria for this first aria of affection for the newborn Jesus? The answer depends partly on how they worked together, which we do not know. The tone of the rage text is evident, but we cannot say whether the parody poet had any idea of the vehemence of Bach's setting—whether, that is, the librettist knew the music as well as the text to be replaced. (It seems likely, though, that the librettist was experienced enough to know what sort of musical setting a text like that would be likely to evoke from a composer.) It is possible that Bach and the poet first looked for a spot for a rage aria in an oratorio for Christmas, but there really isn't one in the first four parts as they planned them. Rage enters only with Herod in parts V and VI, and the music of those parts was derived from a different source, as we have seen. The choice to transform the extant aria radically may have been motivated by a desire to use up the music of the source compositions, whatever it took to do so.

It is worth recalling, though, that once again, the history of the piece is hidden from the listener to the *Christmas Oratorio*—even doubly so, because not only does a listener typically not know the model, but it also has been fully transformed. This example is of technical interest and a starting point for thinking about Bach's parody technique and its significance, not an interpretive tool for the new liturgical work.

We can return to the question posed at the start. What do we do with our knowledge of the parody origin of so much of the *Christmas Oratorio*? If we want to focus on what is audible in the music, then "Bereite dich, Zion" presents a particular challenge, because almost every distinguishing characteristic of the model aria has been altered beyond recognition. Everything, that is, except the notes, and this paradoxical fact might be the key to understanding what is stylistically important in early-eighteenth-century music. The affect, character, associations, and meanings of a movement, liturgical or secular, depend on many features. Successful parodies rely as much on stylistic markers as they do on seemingly fundamental compositional elements such as melody or on musical features in isolation. We have to listen to the whole and think beyond the categories of liturgical and secular, parody and original.

FIVE

Listening to the *Christmas Oratorio* with a Calendar

What is the relationship of a musical work to time?

The best tool for understanding the original context of Bach's *Christmas Oratorio* is probably not the autograph score or the original performing parts or the printed libretto. It's a calendar. Much of what is characteristic of the work stems from the dates and places of its first performance under the composer's direction. In modern times, we usually experience the *Christmas Oratorio* as a single work—in a recording or (long) performance or as a musical object to be studied and analyzed as a whole. There is no question that Bach considered it a unified work; his labeling of it as an oratorio makes that clear. But in some ways, that designation was more conceptual than real, because the work's music would have been experienced as a series of events spread over a surprisingly long stretch of time. The liturgical calendar followed in Leipzig and throughout Lutheran Germany governed almost every aspect of religious observance, including the musical adornment of worship, and that calendar turns out to be a useful starting point for thinking about the status of the *Christmas Oratorio* as a single work and for imagining the piece as it was used in Bach's time.

One good way to approach the context of the *Christmas Oratorio* is to recognize that the work was not so much for Christmas itself as for the season more broadly. Christmas was one of the three main feasts of the liturgical year, together with Easter and Pentecost. Their status is reflected in their observance for three days each. The first day of each principal feast was marked by the greatest festivity and solemnity, and one can hear this in Bach's compositions for the three days of Christmas in his first three years in Leipzig. (See table 5.1.) The cantatas for Christmas Day are the most musically elaborate and celebratory, with trumpets and drums in two of the works and horns (in their highest register and most festive manner) and drums in the other (audio examples 5.1a–5.1c) 🔊. The pieces for the second and third days are more modest and conceived on a smaller scale, including the dialogue BWV 57 (mostly involving just a soprano and a bass singer) and BWV 64, which opens with a musically severe setting of a piece of abstract doctrine (audio examples 5.2a–5.2c and 5.3a–5.3c) 🔊.

From this point of view, the spectacular trumpets-and-drums opening of the first part of the *Christmas Oratorio* (perhaps better, drums-and-trumpets), designed for the first day, makes sense, as does the more modestly scored pastoral part for the second day of Christmas. The portion for the third day, with trumpets and drums once again, is notably more festive than Bach's cantatas for the day and would probably have stood out as unusually elaborate for the occasion. But it uses those instruments only in its opening and closing numbers (the same piece, in fact), a much shorter movement than the long and spectacular opening of part I for Christmas Day, and calls less attention to the trumpets and drums than the arresting opening of part I does.

The music of the *Christmas Oratorio* was almost certainly designed to occupy the same place in the liturgy as the weekly cantata. We do not actually have documentation of this, but it is difficult to imagine another scenario. It makes sense, then, that each unit of the *Christmas Oratorio* is about as long as a substantial church cantata, but they may have stretched the limits for the season. Lorenz Mizler, a writer on music who had studied in Leipzig and probably knew Bach there, wrote that a winter cantata needed to be shorter (around twenty-five minutes) than one for summer because the cold of an unheated church strained listeners and performers alike. Summer cantatas could be eight to ten minutes longer. The parts of the *Christmas Oratorio* range in one recent recording from twenty-one to twenty-seven minutes; this matches Mizler's specification but is actually long compared with most of Bach's cantatas, which tend to be shorter in both the summer and the winter. There are exceptions, and the longer parts of the *Christmas Oratorio* (unsurprisingly, the ones for the major days) are among the most substantial of Bach's liturgical pieces.

There was another calendrical factor involved. Bach, as city music director in Leipzig, was responsible for music at four churches. The third and fourth required only modest music making, so most of his attention was given to the city's main institutions, St. Thomas and St. Nicholas, which he supplied with concerted music (that is, with voices and instruments). Some annual events, such as the musical presentation of the Passion on the afternoon of Good Friday, alternated between the two churches by year. This was a matter of tradition and evidently not obvious to a newcomer; in his first year, Bach confused the church that was supposed to receive a Passion performance and had to print a public notice acknowledging the error.

Generally speaking, though, Bach's musical performances alternated between St. Thomas and St. Nicholas by week throughout the church year. This did not mean that there was no music in the church Bach did not service; there was actually concerted music at both churches each week. This was possible because Bach staffed two ensembles capable of performing this kind of piece. He directed the first group, and his chief musical assistant, usually an advanced pupil or university student known as a prefect, directed the other. The repertory of the first ensemble was dominated by Bach's own compositions, although at various times we know he performed music by others, including a long stretch of cantatas by his cousin Johann Ludwig Bach and (as discovered recently) works from an annual cycle of cantatas by Gottfried Heinrich Stölzel.

As Bach himself wrote, the second group performed music less difficult than the first, but we know essentially nothing about its repertory. The only direct evidence we have of the participation of members of the second ensemble comes in Bach's performances of Passion settings on Good Friday. The availability of its musicians along with those of the first choir allowed him to deploy larger forces: a few more voices beyond his usual four and, in the case of the *St. Matthew Passion*, a few more instruments as well. (How Bach did this and the musical and conceptual consequences are discussed in detail in my earlier book, *Hearing Bach's Passions*. See Suggestions for Further Reading and Listening.)

On the very highest feasts, there was an expectation of the top level of concerted music in both principal churches, so Bach's first ensemble performed at the main service in one church in the morning and at the other for its afternoon service. One these days, the second ensemble presumably performed at the opposite church, swapping with the first between services. We can imagine the members of each ensemble walking the quarter mile between St. Thomas and St. Nicholas across central Leipzig, carrying instruments and music, perhaps meeting up in the central market square.

The relative solemnity and festivity of the days of Christmas and the implications for musical performance in Leipzig are reflected in the performance history of the *Christmas Oratorio*. (See table 5.2.) On Christmas Day and the second day of the feast, Bach's music was heard in both churches. (We know this from the original printed text of the work, which specifies the church or churches at which each part of the *Oratorio* was heard.) Tellingly, the third day saw a performance only at the principal service in the morning (and thus at only one of the churches), because this lesser feast did not call for an afternoon service. In the year of the *Christmas Oratorio*'s first performance, the rotation of church music put Bach's composition and his ensemble in St. Nicholas on the morning of the first day and in St. Thomas on the morning of the second, with afternoon performances at the other church on those days. On the third day, Bach's ensemble was heard only in the morning, that year at St. Nicholas, and only in that church because there was no afternoon service.

This has implications for how the *Christmas Oratorio* was heard, because Leipzigers typically attended one church or the other. The well-to-do (meaning most of the congregants) rented family pews, guaranteeing them a seat in keeping with their standing in the community. A regular attender of St. Nicholas would have heard all three of the first parts of the *Oratorio*, but those who worshipped at St. Thomas would not have heard the third part. That is, half the members of Bach's congregations would have heard just the first and second parts of the *Christmas Oratorio* in 1734–35 during the three days of Christmas.

All these considerations—the relative festivity of particular liturgical days and the consequences for multiple performances—also applied to the fourth, fifth, and sixth parts of the *Christmas Oratorio,* because the celebration of Christmas (and the work) extended beyond the three-day feast itself beginning on December 25 to the twelve days ending with Epiphany on January 6. Part IV was designed for New Year's Day, celebrated in various Christian denominations, including German Lutheranism of the eighteenth century, as the feast of Jesus's circumcision in recognition of the eighth day in the life of a Jewish newborn. New Year's was celebrated in Leipzig with great festivity, nearly on the level of the first day of Christmas; three of four of Bach's cantatas for the occasion use trumpets and drums (audio examples 5.4a–5.4d) ⬤. The texts of many New Year's works are words of praise, probably to symbolically begin the new year with an act of devotion. Part IV of the *Christmas Oratorio*, for this day, calls for horns but not drums, making it somewhat less festive but still marked by musical opulence. The first line of its text speaks of thanks and praise, in keeping with typical New Year's observance.

Part VI of the *Oratorio* is for Epiphany (January 6), celebrated almost as elaborately as the first day of Christmas and New Year's Day. Neither of Bach's surviving cantatas for the day uses trumpets and drums, as this part of the *Oratorio* does, so it stands out as somewhat more elaborate. We can note that "Sie werden aus Saba alle kommen" BWV 65, with horns, recorders and oboes da caccia, is particularly richly scored (audio examples 5.5a and 5.5b) 🔊. Both part VI and part IV (for New Year's Day) were heard in both principal churches, as was probably the case with typical annual cantatas for the day in keeping with the festivity of New Year's Day and of Epiphany.

In between is part V, for the Sunday after New Year's, in some ways the most complicated liturgically. This was not a particularly important event on the church calendar; in fact, it was dispensable. New Year's Day and Epiphany are, of course, fixed dates on the calendar, but they fall on different days of the week from year to year, just as someone's birthday does. That means that in some years there is a Sunday between New Year's and Epiphany, but in some years there is not. If Christmas and New Year's (exactly a week apart) both fall on a Wednesday, Thursday, Friday, or Saturday, there is a Sunday between New Year's and Epiphany, but if they fall on Sunday, Monday, or Tuesday, this feast is not observed.

When it did occur, the Sunday after New Year's was celebrated with concerted music from Bach's ensemble at only one of Leipzig's two principal churches, just like the third day of Christmas, not at both because there was no afternoon service at which a repeat performance could take place. We have only one cantata by Bach that is certainly for this occasion, a relatively modestly scored work that matches the status of the day in the liturgical hierarchy (audio example 5.6) 🔊. Pretty much the same considerations apply to the Sunday after Christmas, present only in some liturgical years and celebrated with a cantata at only one church with modest festivity. Two cantatas for Leipzig by Bach survive for this date (audio examples 5.7a and 5.7b) 🔊.

The low status of the Sunday after New Year's meant that only one of the two Leipzig congregations heard that day's part of the *Christmas Oratorio*. The rotation in 1734–35 put the performance at St. Nicholas; this part was not heard at St. Thomas. The two congregations thus heard different *Christmas Oratorio*s. Listeners at St. Nicholas heard all six parts, but those at St. Thomas heard only parts I, II, IV, and VI. (See table 5.2.)

Did this matter? Apparently not to Bach—or at least the situation was tolerable. It might make us think, though, about what it means to listen to the "whole" *Christmas Oratorio* today. Does that necessarily mean all six parts in order? Or does the St. Thomas sequence

I–II–IV–VI count, too? We might be seeing here a difference between an abstract ideal of a work and its practical realization, although it rarely makes sense to imagine that there is such a thing as an ideal version of a church composition by Bach. This was practical music put to practical use, and abstracting it quickly leads to interpretive trouble, because we have to attempt to read Bach's mind in imagining what the work means outside its utilitarian value. But the contrast between a complete work and the way it was sometimes heard is difficult to avoid here, and there may well be an ideal *Christmas Oratorio* and a practical one.

The problem might be even worse, because there is a further complication in the Sunday after Christmas. Like the Sunday after New Year's, this liturgical date might or might not exist; it is present in the calendar only if Christmas Day falls on a Monday, Tuesday, Wednesday, or Thursday, allowing for a Sunday (not counting the second and third days of Christmas) before New Year's Day arrives on January 1. (There was no Sunday after Christmas in 1734–35, when the *Christmas Oratorio* was first heard.) This could actually matter in relation to the *Christmas Oratorio*, because the observation of this Sunday would interrupt the successive presentation of the six parts of the *Christmas Oratorio* by inserting a cantata between part III on the third day of Christmas and part IV on New Year's Day. (We have three cantatas for this day from Bach, in fact.) It is difficult to say whether that would really be significant, because we are talking about twenty-to-thirty-minute musical performances separated by many days. If hearing another Bach church work between parts of the *Christmas Oratorio* is a problem, it is a conceptual one.

The issue arises because scholars have wondered whether the *Christmas Oratorio* was usable only in liturgical years that match the 1734–35 Christmas season precisely; that is, those in which Christmas and New Year's fall on a Friday or Saturday, producing a Sunday after New Year's Day but not one after Christmas. (See table 5.3.) Starting in 1734–35 and through the 1749–50 Christmas season, Bach's last, there were three more years that had sequences matching the design of the *Christmas Oratorio* and twelve that did not, either lacking a Sunday after New Year's or adding a Sunday after Christmas. Only the seasons 1739–40, 1744–45, and 1745–46 match exactly. Was the *Christmas Oratorio* reperformed after its first hearing, and was it limited to years whose calendar (and sequence of feasts) matched its original design? If it was not restricted in that way, does that imply various possible presentations of the work's parts?

We know that during a period of intense compositional work in his first three years in Leipzig, Bach developed a working repertory of church music and reperformed pieces over the course of his service there for the next twenty-five years; he occasionally added to this repertory but not with the regularity of his first three years. We can usually date the composition and first performance of a work from features of the original sources, when they survive: Bach's handwriting, the participation of the changing roster of copyists who assisted him, and the paper they used for composing and for copying. But we know about reperformances only when they left documentary traces—additional or replacement performing parts, revisions such as substituting movements (particularly in the Passion settings), or other interventions. It was perfectly possible for Bach to pull a set of parts off the shelf, perform a work precisely as it stood, and then return it to the cabinets in the cantor's composing room on the top floor of the St. Thomas School without leaving a trace. We assume this happened often but, of course, cannot be sure from the appearance of surviving materials.

We can say with certainty that the original performing parts for the *Christmas Oratorio* were all copied in connection with the first performances in 1734–35. There is only one revision that might point to a later use of the parts: additions (at least partly in Bach's own hand) to one of the two basso continuo parts. They were both originally copied as a regular continuo parts, probably intended for a cello or a violone (double bass), Bach's usual instruments on the continuo line in addition to a keyboard. That keyboard was usually an organ, for which a third distinct and identifiable part exists. At some point, one of the two continuo parts was altered in a way that would have allowed it to be used by a harpsichord player, presumably in place of organ.

This probably took place after 1734–35, but we cannot say precisely when, other than that it was during Bach's lifetime. The preparation of a substitute continuo part for harpsichord in place of organ (some think in addition to it) crops up frequently in Bach's performing materials and usually points to a reperformance of a work under new circumstances. We cannot be certain, but that might be the case with part IV of the *Christmas Oratorio*, the unit for New Year's Day—but only part IV, to judge from this evidence, because this change was made only in that part of the *Oratorio*. If Bach had reason to use harpsichord in one church on that date, we would probably expect him to have done the same with other parts of the *Oratorio* when they were performed there that year and also to find that he produced analogous harpsichord parts for those *Oratorio* parts. But he evidently did not, and this could mean that at some point, Bach used part IV on its own, implying that he sometimes extracted individual parts of the *Oratorio*.

All this matters for the way we listen to and think about the work. If we attend a performance of just the first three parts, are we hearing half the piece or a form in which Bach might have used its music on the first three days of Christmas? Is it acceptable to leave out part V, emulating a year in which there was neither a Sunday after Christmas nor one after New Year's (1735–36, 1740–41, and 1746–47 in Bach's time)? And when we consider the work's musical, narrative, and theological dimensions, do we have to think about all six parts, or should we consider other permutations? It does not seem out of the question, for example, that years in which there was no Sunday after New Year's, Bach might have used part V on the Sunday after Christmas, although that would have put the gospel narrative out of order.

There is no doubt that Bach thought of the *Christmas Oratorio* as a single work; the singular "oratorio" he used several times in its sources demonstrates this, as does his careful numbering of the "parts of the oratorio." But we need to consider whether the only way to think about a piece is in its abstract and perhaps ideal complete form or whether the work as heard in performance might be just as ripe for analysis and interpretation.

What makes the *Christmas Oratorio* a single work, anyway? One important element is the more or less continuous narrative that runs through the six parts. In fact, the narrative element, heard mostly in the words of an evangelist but also in occasional direct speech of groups and individuals, is what makes the piece an oratorio at all. It shares this designation among Bach's works with the *Ascension Oratorio* BWV 11 (also with scriptural narration in the voice of a tenor). Bach's Passion settings are of the same type, although we have no original source that uses the word *oratorio*, probably because the designation "Passion" took precedence. Bach's *Easter Oratorio* BWV 249 does not, in fact, have direct scriptural narration or identified characters. (As it happens, though, the cantata Bach revised to produce it consisted entirely of poetic statements by named characters in the Easter story. Maybe he continued to regard the text as direct speech and thus called the revised work an oratorio.)

The narrative thread of the *Christmas Oratorio* was the result of some careful calculation by Bach and his librettist. The starting point was presumably the gospel readings specified for each of the feasts for which the parts of the *Oratorio* were designed, but Bach and his collaborator did not adhere strictly to them. (See table 5.4.) The readings assigned to the first two days of Christmas are a continuous narration of the nativity drawn from Luke's gospel; the reading for the third day abandons the narrative in favor of prophecy drawn from the first chapters of John's gospel. This reading is distinctly unsuited to an oratorio, which is supposed to narrate a story, and that feature probably played a role in the design of Bach's work. The first three parts of the *Christmas Oratorio*, for consecutive days, distributes the narration of the nativity over three days, displacing the second day's reading to the third day's music and distributing the gospel read on the first day over the first two musical performances. (Bach and his librettist skip one verse, Luke 2:2, which names the governor of Syria at the time, perhaps because it is of little narrative interest. The verse has been the subject of debate, because Luke's dates do not align with historical records, but this might have nothing to do with its omission here.)

The loosened ties between gospel readings and the scriptural texts set to music in the parts of the *Oratorio* are a reminder that the parts are not cantatas, which typically draw on the scriptural readings assigned to their day, although they behave like them textually and musically. The rearranging of the gospel portions does have the result of binding the first three parts of the *Christmas Oratorio* closely together by continuous narrative, the defining feature of oratorio. There are also musical ties that invite us to hear these three parts as a unit. Instrumentation is perhaps the most audible, with the first and third days calling for trumpets and drums (in the home key of D major that typically goes with those instruments), surrounding the pastorally scored second day, with its multiple oboes and transverse flutes. A desire on the part of Bach and his librettist to create this three-day sequence probably explains the unusually elaborate music they designed for the third day of Christmas, which in some respects matches the music of the first day and (as discussed earlier) exceeds the usual festivity of the day.

Each of these three parts presents passages of gospel narrative with poetic and hymnic commentary; this is the fundamental structure of every early-eighteenth-century gospel oratorio. Each is framed by an opening movement (a chorus in the first and third parts, a pastoral sinfonia in the second) and by a closing setting of a chorale stanza based on a simple harmonization. The pastoral sinfonia seems to have been something of a tradition in eighteenth-century works that treat the nativity. The first part of Handel's *Messiah* has one, labeled "Pifa" (meaning a piece for woodwinds, as in the word "fife") in the equivalent spot (audio example 5.8a and 5.8b) ◐. The passages of gospel narrative in the *Christmas Oratorio* are interrupted for reflective commentary in the form of instrumentally accompanied recitatives and arias setting new poetry and for hymn stanzas, with those hymns sometimes combined with new poetry in hybrid movements in which the two texts interact.

Part III ends with a repeat of its opening chorus, after the "concluding" chorale. This appears to have been Bach's idea and is not specified in the libretto, which ends with the chorale text. The reappearance of the trumpets and drums in this movement represents another elevation of the musical festivity of the day but also solves a musical problem. The librettist specified a chorale stanza whose tune, "Wir Christenleut," is in a minor key. Each part of the *Christmas Oratorio* is of a type that conventionally places fully scored movements at the beginning and at the end, in the same key and using identical scoring (the full forces of the work). Sticking to this model, which he followed in all the other parts of the *Oratorio*, meant that Bach could not begin part III with a major-key trumpets-and-drums movement and end it with a minor-mode chorale harmonization, because trumpets did not ordinarily play in minor-key movements or in much of anything outside D major. Bach solved the problem by repeating the short opening chorus at the end; there are many eighteenth-century pieces, including a number by Bach, that end with a return of their opening movement (audio examples 5.9a and 5.9b) 🔊. An alternative would have been a particularly elaborate setting that allowed the composer to project both the major key of trumpet music and the minor key of the hymn; we have pieces by Bach that do similar things, but he did not attempt it here.

The fifth and sixth parts of the *Oratorio* work together in almost the same way as the first three. Here the gospel reading assigned to Epiphany is spread over the two last parts, entirely displacing the reading specified for the Sunday after New Year the week before. That reading would likely have been problematic anyway because it occurs out of narrative sequence; this probably did not matter for the general liturgical observance of the Christmas season, but would have stood out in a narrated musical work like an oratorio. As in the first three parts, passages of gospel narrative are interrupted for accompanied recitatives, arias, and chorale stanzas that reflect on ideas and images in the gospel words. And each part ends with a chorale that draws on the simplest kind of harmonization. The last movement of the final part is more elaborate; Bach builds a full ritornello movement, with trumpets and drums, but embedded in the elaborate and celebratory frame is a plain chorale harmonization; part IV ends similarly.

Parts V and VI, which present a continuous narrative, are less clearly linked to each other than the first three. They do not share instrumentation and are centered around closely related but distinct keys. In fact, they are connected more by their gospel text than they are musically. The last part does represent a return to the key and instrumentation of the opening part of the *Christmas Oratorio*, with its D major and trumpets and drums. In this sense, the final part rounds off the whole *Oratorio* in much the same way that opening and closing movements frame an individual eighteenth-century work.

Part IV for New Year's Day is different. It was probably going to be different from the start, because the gospel reading for the day consists of exactly one verse describing Jesus's circumcision and naming. After an opening chorus, that verse is presented in full; the rest of the cantata is entirely poetic (mostly new verse, with some hymn texts), a series of reflections on Jesus's name, including a final choral that repeats that name at the start of every line. One of Bach's other cantatas for New Year's Day, "Herr Gott, dich loben wir" BWV 16, takes up the same theme of the name; the others are about the new year itself and offer words of praise to begin the year.

That it is naming and not circumcision that is the focus in the *Christmas Oratorio* and in the cantatas for New Year's Day is typical, perhaps motivated partly by a theological perspective that deemphasized the ritual prescriptions of the Hebrew Testament. There are cantatas from the period, though, whose texts do dwell on the act itself, typically seeing the blood shed in that rite as prefiguring the blood spilled on the cross. (That sort of imagery might be one reason this repertory is not performed much today.) There is a hint of this interpretation in the *Oratorio*'s quotation of a chorale stanza about the cross in the third movement of part IV, a text that would probably have been heard in this light.

The lack of further narration and the absence of direct speech of characters and groups determine the nature of part IV; it is more contemplative and reflective than the others. Each part of the *Christmas Oratorio* is capable of standing on its own, and each is musically well formed by eighteenth-century criteria and textually complete. But part IV might be the most independent of all, with its almost entirely reflective character, most divorced from the continuous narration and arguably less dependent on the other parts through the connecting narrative. Maybe this explains the possibility that Bach used it individually at some point.

In a couple of respects, part IV is also musically distinct. Its festive instrumentation calls on horns, not trumpets and drums, and with that choice comes a key (F major, as it happens) that would have been heard as musically distant from the rest of the work—certainly from the framing and central D-major parts. Even listeners who have no idea about the key of a work can clearly hear the very different worlds of trumpet music and horn music. The characteristics of the text have further consequences; without the alternation of gospel text and interpolated commentary, found otherwise throughout the *Oratorio*, the libretto creates dialogue and interaction between texts and voices in other ways, including two movements in which a chorale text combines with free poetry set as accompanied recitative and in the dialogue aria "Flösst, mein Heiland," which adds an echo voice.

But this part of the *Christmas Oratorio* is exceptional; overall, the work is characterized by its continuous narrative spread over twelve days in six units. This is most unusual for a narrative work of any kind, certainly for a musical composition. Textually and by the experience of the music, the work underlines an important aspect of the observation of the Christmas season: its principal feasts do not simply narrate but rather reenact Jesus's first days. Christmas Day marks the birth, of course; eight days later, both in the narration and in the actual time of the observation, come the circumcision and naming; and twelve days later, in both senses, the visit of the Magi is one of several events commemorated on Epiphany. The narrative extends literally over the period of time it narrates. In this sense, the *Christmas Oratorio* is not just spread over twelve days; it encompasses them.

Where did Bach get the idea for a narrative oratorio spread over six performances in twelve days? Since the reappearance of the *Christmas Oratorio* in the middle of the nineteenth century, commentators have sought models and have proposed some likely sounding antecedents in an attempt to make Bach's work the pinnacle of a tradition. This is in keeping with a widely cultivated image of the composer. A popular biography called Bach "the culmination of an era," and a standard history of Protestant church music marked the beginning of church music's decline as the year 1750, when Bach died. This view all but demanded antecedents that Bach supposedly brought to perfection, and the *Christmas Oratorio* was no exception.

The most inviting comparison has always been the *Actus musicus for Christmas* by Johann Schelle, one of Bach's predecessors as *Thomascantor* and Leipzig city music director. This is a lovely piece worth hearing, but from a textual point of view, the comparison with Bach's *Oratorio* is only approximate, as the text of Schelle's work (after an opening liturgical formula) is drawn entirely from gospel passages and chorale stanzas and lacks poetic commentary. It is thus not an oratorio in the modern sense, unsurprisingly for a work probably from the 1680s. Perhaps this distinction is not essential, though. The work is in three parts, and its gospel narrative consists of the readings from Luke specified for the first and second of the three days of Christmas. It has been repeatedly proposed—assumed, actually—that the work was performed over several days, divided so that a hypothetical first day's unit presents the gospel reading for the first day of Christmas and the supposed second and third days split the remaining text (the portion read on the second day).

The parallel to Bach's work is clear, but there is a problem: there is no evidence for performance of this work over multiple days. Even if it is liturgically plausible that Schelle's work was heard over three days, the brevity of the musical setting makes this unlikely; part II lasts approximately two and a half minutes and seems unlikely to have stood on its own. To all appearances, Schelle's composition was a single-day piece, and its supposed performance over multiple days is a modern idea, not something documented or even hinted at in the sources. I think this aspect of the work was foisted on it to make it look more like a model for Bach's *Christmas Historia* by one of his predecessors.

Almost inevitably, Heinrich Schütz's *Christmas Oratorio* has likewise been proposed as a model for Bach's, including with respect to multiday presentation. Again, the work is only loosely comparable because it consists entirely of gospel narration, with no interpolated commentary. But as with Schelle's work, the real problem is the division of the work over several days—or, rather, the lack of it, as there is no evidence that the work was divided at all, let alone over multiple days. In fact, aside from a couple of works that presented a narrative over the first and second days of Christmas—following the two days' assigned gospel readings—there is no evidence of any Christmas works spread over multiple days.

This appears to be an invented tradition, concocted in the hope of finding connections between Bach's *Christmas Oratorio* and works by predecessors, especially iconic ones such as Schütz. Scholars have been eager to suggest a line of development of Christmas oratorios, particularly in a popular or supposedly folklike vein (labels attached to Bach's work in the nineteenth century, as discussed in chapter 6), running from the earliest flowering of Lutheran sacred music in the early seventeenth century through to Bach in the eighteenth. Even leaving aside the dubious concept of musical "development," there does not appear to be a line of multiday Christmas pieces before Bach's largely because there are hardly any such pieces at all, and maybe there is none. Bach's *Christmas Oratorio* was not the culmination of a tradition, because there was no tradition.

Historians are not the only ones to invent antecedents and parallels. Recordings of seasonal music by Bach's contemporaries Christoph Graupner and Gottfried Heinrich Stölzel have recently been packaged as "Christmas oratorios." This probably helps sell CDs but misrepresents the repertory, because the works on these recordings are Christmas-season liturgical cantatas, mostly without narration, put in order as if they were direct parallels to the parts of Bach's work. Their composers and librettists never considered them oratorios or multiple parts of anything other than annual cycles of cantatas. Bach—or at least a modern view of Bach—appears to have reached back in time to influence the compositions of his contemporaries and even his predecessors. This is a poor way to write history or to understand the context of the *Christmas Oratorio*.

We can do a little better by appreciating the likely influence of the so-called *Abendmusiken* presented in the northern city of Lübeck, public concerts that were among the first of their kind anywhere. Under the direction of Dieterich Buxtehude, organist at the Marienkirche there, the *Abendmusiken* presented (mostly) dramatic oratorios spanning multiple days, initially on the second and third Sundays in Advent and eventually extending to five Sundays from approximately 1681. There are clear points of contact between the *Abendmusiken* and Bach's *Christmas Oratorio*, particularly in the performance of each over multiple days, but the parallel goes only so far, because the Lübeck events were nonliturgical. Their librettos also soon abandoned biblical narrative for poetry and emphasized reflection and dialogue over continuous storytelling.

Bach himself experienced the *Abendmusiken* in the fall of 1705 on his famous trip to Lübeck to visit Buxtehude. But the *Abendmusiken* that year were not narrative; instead, they presented allegorical representations of mourning and celebration of the deceased and new emperors, respectively. Bach might have known the text or music of later narrative works, but his own experience in Lübeck did not supply a direct model for the *Christmas Oratorio*.

In fact, there is a more direct comparison with the *Christmas Oratorio*: Lutheran Passion performances spread over multiple days. There turn out to have been more of these, concentrated in Saxony and Thuringia, than has been recognized, involving both newly composed works and adapted pieces, heard in both liturgical and devotional contexts. It is paradoxical that this model should have been relatively unnoticed by scholars, because so much of the *Christmas Oratorio*'s modern reception has been in relation to Passion music (as discussed in chapter 6).

Each of these multiday Passion settings starts with a crucifixion narrative but usually not one that presents the words of an individual gospel, as in Bach's settings. Instead, most use a combination of gospels that incorporates events and dialogue from the four tellings of the Passion story in the New Testament. This kind of text was known as a "harmonized gospel"; the term refers not to musical harmony but to the attempt to reconcile the somewhat different presentations by the four evangelists. The best-known Passion narrative of this type, dating from the earliest years of the Reformation, was a text compiled by theologian Johann Bugenhagen in the sixteenth century.

The fondness for harmonized gospels had a couple of consequences. One was length; fitting in all the detail offered by the four evangelists yields a very long Passion narrative, which lent itself to division into multiple parts. The other was Bugenhagen's own division of the story into five units, which corresponded in turn to the traditional division of the Passion narrative into "acts": scenes of Jesus in the garden, before the high priests, before Pontius Pilate, on the cross, and in the grave. A long, quasi-dramatically divided narrative was a natural for distribution over more than one day.

This was particularly true because the liturgical calendar provided periods of preparation for the commemoration of the Passion story. The earliest multiday musical Passion we know about (from the court of Rudolstadt from the year 1688 and perhaps earlier) divided the Passion narrative into six parts presented serially over the week leading to Easter: Palm Sunday; the Monday, Tuesday, and Wednesday of Holy Week; Maundy Thursday; and Good Friday (on which the crucifixion itself was narrated). Each portion of the narrative was introduced, concluded, and occasionally interrupted by hymns and new poetry reflecting on the events. This, of course, became the model for Lutheran Passion settings, including Bach's.

The composition from Rudolstadt was cited by its composer as a single work in multiple parts, showing that he thought of it as unified. (The music is lost.) Other multiday Passion settings followed the same general principle but extended the time span over which the story was presented, distributing the narrative over nine, ten, and even twelve days in a span of weeks. This was accomplished by pushing the first units back into the even longer preparatory season known as Lent, which lasted approximately six weeks and culminated in Holy Week from Palm Sunday through Good Friday. Performances of multiday Passions typically began with the first or second Sunday in Lent and continued on each of its Sundays and into Holy Week.

We know of performances like this in Rudolstadt, Nuremberg, and Eisenach (a work that might have been composed by Georg Philipp Telemann), at the small court of Schleiz, and in Erfurt. The works span at least the years 1688 to 1750, and the closer one gets to the years of Bach's employment in Leipzig, the more the librettos resemble those of Bach's Passions, with modern poetry offering commentary and reflection designed to be set as recitatives and arias. Unfortunately, none of the musical settings of these multiday Passions survives; what we know comes from printed texts.

The later Passions of this kind do not set literal gospel text. Instead, their narrative skeleton is a poetic paraphrase of New Testament language, likewise drawn from all four evangelists, reflecting a fondness for harmonized tellings. This poetic mode of presentation became intensely fashionable in the first decade of the eighteenth century, partly because the poetic narratives are even more explicitly emotional in their telling of the story than the gospels and thus aligned with tastes in religious thought and expression.

In fact, two of the multiday settings use the earliest and most famous poetic Passion text, Barthold Heinrich Brockes's poem set by Telemann, Handel, Reinhard Keiser, Johann Mattheson, and many others. Brockes's very baroque title was "Jesus, martyred and dying for the sins of the world, presented in poetry, from the four evangelists," a formulation that makes clear both the focus on the vivid depiction of events and the reliance on all four gospels. This text deeply influenced Bach and his Passion librettists; it was the source of arias in Bach's *St. John Passion* and the model for the free poetry in the *St. Matthew Passion*.

The use of this text for multiday Passions is significant, because the Brockes text was unified and integrated, originally meant to be set as a single musical unit heard in one sitting. Two eighteenth-century settings are known to have divided it over multiple days; in at least one of them, the performers split up an extant setting (Reinhard Keiser's) by adding chorales as framing movements, making each unit self-sufficient. The divisions were made in a way that lent each unit some narrative and even quasi-dramatic unity by isolating the speech of individual characters (in addition to Jesus) in each unit. Unfortunately, we do not have the musical text of this version (although Keiser's splendid setting survives in its original form, without the added movements that made its multiday performance possible), but the surviving printed text shows how the divisions were made.

Overall, multiday performance of continuous Passion narratives was a familiar practice in central Germany. It is probable that Bach knew of these divided Passion performances; they took place in towns with which he had strong connections, particularly through his musically active family members.

And this is the context in which we need to view this aspect of his *Christmas Oratorio*, which has many features in common with the multiday Passion performances. It presents a continuous gospel narrative heard in six parts spread over twelve days. It is partly aligned with daily readings but redistributes gospel material over the available dates. It constitutes an integral work but is divided into self-sufficient units articulated with commentary movements, including concluding chorale stanzas. And it exists both as a unified work and as a series of free-standing parts, just as multiday Passions do.

If the idea of a multiday oratorio interested Bach, his options were limited. In particular, a divided Passion oratorio was ruled out by Leipzig's observance of the *tempus clausum* (closed time), which dictated that no concerted church music was heard during Lent, the six-week preparatory period for the observation of the Passion. After the first Sunday in Lent and continuing until Easter, there was no cantata or organ music heard in the Leipzig churches. The only exceptions were the feast of the Annunciation (March 25, which fell during Lent or Holy Week in most years but not all) and, starting in the early 1720s, performance of a concerted Passion at Good Friday vespers. Throughout Lutheran Germany, Holy Week was known, in fact, as the *stille Woche* (the quiet week). The restrictions on church music were taken seriously and in many towns extended to bans on luxury, recreation, and celebration in nonchurch life as well. This represented an extension of the already strict sumptuary laws that dictated the propriety of everyday behavior according to class and social standing, as well as according to the liturgical calendar.

There were some musical consequences of the observation of the *tempus clausum*. One was that the resumption of music on Easter was particularly striking, especially with its almost obligatory blaze of trumpets and drums. Another is that Lent was a relatively quiet period for eighteenth-century church musicians in places that observed the *tempus clausum*, breaking the relentless demand for weekly service music. This is why the only Lenten cantatas we have from Bach (aside from those for the first Sunday, before the closed time took effect) are from his earlier years, before he moved to Leipzig. The respite appears to have offered Bach and his assistants the opportunity to prepare the performing materials for large works such as the Passion settings.

In other places, though, the opposite was true. For example, the music director and performers in Hamburg, which did not observe a closed time, presented not only the usual rotation of weekly music in the five churches for which they were responsible but also approximately a dozen Passion performances during Lent. This was the lot of Telemann, music director there from 1721 to 1767, and his successor Carl Philipp Emanuel Bach, who served from 1768 to 1788, and it must have been exhausting. (It should be noted, though, that the Passion settings they performed were much shorter—about an hour—than J. S. Bach's surviving works.)

There appears to have been no room in Leipzig for any exception to the ban on Lenten performances besides the musically subdued Good Friday Passion and the one Marian feast. A multiday Passion setting was thus not possible, because the days of Holy Week and the Lenten Sundays were ruled out. In any event, Bach appears to have had a free hand in presenting as long a Passion oratorio as he pleased, as the dimensions of the *St. Matthew Passion* demonstrate. There was limited opportunity for an oratorio of any kind, because there was no liturgical place for such a setting in Leipzig beyond the usual weekly cantata. The concerted Passion, for example, was heard at the vesper service, not the principal morning worship on Good Friday. Bach's oratorios for Easter and Ascension Day are both on the scale of long individual cantatas and were presumably presented in the usual slot for a cantata.

A nativity oratorio presented a similar challenge. There was no liturgical place for such a piece. There was also no possibility of backing it up into the days or weeks before Christmas, in parallel to Lenten Passion performances elsewhere or in emulation of *Abendmusiken* presented in Lübeck during Advent, the four-week preparatory season before Christmas. This is because Leipzig also observed Advent as a *tempus clausum*: after the first Sunday in Advent, there was no church music until the first day of Christmas, marked (like Easter) with particularly festive compositions. There was simply no outlet for an oratorio at Christmas, at least not one much longer than a usual cantata. The six-part design of the *Christmas Oratorio* made it possible for Bach to present a long musical setting of the Christmas narrative.

Composing such a work meant striking a balance between the necessity of the parts standing on their own and a desire to create a single musical work. In this regard, the multiday Passion offered a model. Without surviving music, we do not know how close Bach's solution was to the one struck in those works, but seen against the background of multiday Passion performances, the features of his *Christmas Oratorio* come into focus. Each part is constructed as a musically closed unit; the parts of Bach's *Oratorio* are unified by key (identical in first and last movements, related in internal ones) and by instrumentation. Each follows the trajectory of many of Bach's weekly cantatas, with a large opening movement for all the forces and a concluding movement likewise using all the voices and instruments but consisting of a simple chorale harmonization or its elaboration. (The third day's part of the *Oratorio* adds a repetition of the opening chorus, as mentioned earlier, but this was not part of the original design.) In this sense, each part stands on its own and resembles a weekly cantata in many respects.

But the six parts are linked by continuous narrative in the voice of a tenor singing the words of an evangelist. The narrative portions are continuous in parts I–IV and in parts V and VI, deviating from the assigned daily gospel readings, presumably in the interest of connection. The opening and closing parts match in key and instrumentation (at least in the prominent use of trumpets and drums; they differ a little in that the first part calls for transverse flutes and bassoon not heard in the last). The final part ends with movements that not only conclude the day's music but also bring the entire *Oratorio* to a close. The last is the most elaborate of all the concluding chorale movements, a full ritornello treatment that prominently includes trumpets and drums. The penultimate movement is a recitative joined by each singer one by one, a sort of piece borrowed from contemporary opera that signals the close of a work. (Bach's *St. Matthew Passion* makes a similar gesture in its next-to-last movement, "Nun ist der Herr zu Ruh gebracht," in which each voice of the first chorus is heard in turn; several of Bach's secular dramas do the same.)

There are additional ways in which the *Christmas Oratorio* as a whole behaves like a typical composition by Bach. To give just one example, the distribution of arias among the four voice types is characteristic. Each voice is assigned three or four arias, including a duet and one with an echo. (The number of accompanied recitatives varies a great deal more.) The even distribution, typical of Bach's large-scale works, is partly a result of the distribution of solo music in the source compositions from which he drew his parodies, but it contributes to the sense that the *Christmas Oratorio* is a single work.

That might be a feature, though, that makes itself felt only in a continuous performance of all six parts of the *Oratorio*. The modern experience of listening to all of Bach's music is very different from that in his time, but the *Christmas Oratorio* is probably uniquely different in one important respect. It is not just that we often hear the piece (or its first half) in one sitting, giving us effectively Bach's vision of the *Oratorio* as an integral work, a perspective not available to eighteenth-century listeners. Rather, its very relationship to time has changed. Perhaps we should follow along with the next performance not with a libretto or a score in our lap but with a calendar.

SIX

The *Christmas Oratorio* in the Shadow of Bach's Passions

How shall I receive you?

Modern interest in Bach as a composer of church music owes a great deal to one celebrated moment: the 1829 Berlin performance of a version of his *St. Matthew Passion* under the musical direction of Felix Mendelssohn. The context was a concert, not a liturgy. and the performing organization was the Berlin Sing-Akademie, a bourgeois amateur society that had been founded in the late eighteenth century to promote the private study of great music from the past for the artistic and moral edification of its middle-class members. The public performance of the *Passion* was a departure for the organization, marking a gradual move from private rehearsal, largely of Bach's music, to public performances. The effect was sensational, beginning the restoration of Bach's large-scale concerted vocal music to the repertory.

To the concert repertory, that is; this music had become liturgically unuseable soon after Bach's death. His sons did perform his church compositions in their professional duties. Wilhelm Friedemann Bach used his father's music in Halle, sometimes presenting entire cantatas and reworking others. His most famous adaptation was the arrangement of two movements from "Ein feste Burg ist unser Gott" BWV 80, which he fitted with newly written Latin texts and to which he added trumpets and drums, most likely for a ceremony celebrating the end of a war in the 1760s (audio example 6.1) . (In the nineteenth century, those trumpet-and-drum movements were mistakenly edited back into J. S. Bach's cantata, which never used the instruments, and they are still sometimes heard today as if they were original.)

Carl Philipp Emanuel Bach made use of his father's Passion music, incorporating an abbreviated gospel narrative from the *St. Matthew Passion*, adapted for a single chorus rather than a double choir, into a Passion setting in the late 1760s when he began his position as chief church musician in Hamburg, and adapting the closing chorus of the *St. John Passion* for another Passion setting. J. S. Bach's successors in his Leipzig position, Gottlob Harrer and Johann Friedrich Doles, also made some use of Bach's cantatas in the years after Bach's death.

But not much, because the cantatas were largely unusable, only partly because of their music; it was their texts that created problems. Preferences in religious poetry changed rapidly, making the wild and graphic imagery of recitative and aria texts from the 1710s and 1720s dated and even tasteless. Even hymns became outdated; the second half of the eighteenth century saw almost every hymn text revised to suit modern, more rationalistic sensibilities. The process started during Bach's lifetime; the last version of his *St. John Passion* was heard with revised texts that eliminated some of the more flamboyant language of the originals dating from 1724 and that were based, in turn, on poetry ten years older.

The music by Bach that remained in the Leipzig repertory was his motets, whose almost exclusively biblical and hymn texts made them more verbally timeless. The same was true of Latin church music, whose liturgical text did not date as easily. The *Magnificat* and a Mass movement attributed to Bach were among the earliest of his vocal music published around the turn of the nineteenth century (that the Mass setting was not actually by Bach is not so significant here). The motets were also published right around this time.

By the 1820s, Bach's Passions and other concerted liturgical compositions were historical, and it is no accident that their revival was in concert performances connected with cultural edification, with reverence for the past, and with a sense of that past as a foundation of German nationhood. This was the context of the Sing-Akademie's 1829 performance of the *St. Matthew Passion* and performances of that work and of the *St. John Passion* in Berlin and elsewhere in the years that followed. The Sing-Akademie also revived the *Mass in B Minor*, which had been known to composers (including Haydn and Beethoven) but was not part of public consciousness. One of the *Mass*'s earliest proponents, who sponsored a printed edition of the score, called it "the greatest artwork of all times and all peoples," showing clearly that the veneration of Bach as a master was well under way, but most of the musical public had never heard the work, and it had not yet come to define Bach's image.

The Passions played that role among vocal works, standing alongside the preludes and fugues of the *Well-Tempered Clavier* and a few organ works in representing who Bach was and what he stood for. The Passions, particularly the *St. Matthew Passion*, were valued for elements that nineteenth-century commentators found notable in them. They were serious and weighty, full of labyrinthine harmonies and contrapuntal complexities, tragic, lamenting, dramatic, and morally uplifting. (These features were also cited as the reasons for the music's difficulty for modern listeners, although it should be noted that "difficulty" was not always pejorative, according to an aesthetic came to value it.)

It was against this background that the *Christmas Oratorio* was the last of Bach's major vocal-instrumental works to be rediscovered. As writers on Bach's music encountered the *Christmas Oratorio*, they found it difficult to square with the music of the Passions and with the style they expected from their composer. The *Oratorio*, in contrast to the Passions, was sunny and smiling, simple, and galant—even prompting doubt about Bach's authorship. (C. P. E. Bach was suggested as a possible compiler of the material.) Its lighter style, aligning better with secular music, was a source of puzzlement.

And then commentators discovered the parody origin of much of the *Christmas Oratorio* in actual secular compositions. This created multiple problems, if not a crisis. Not only was there the lighter musical style of the *Oratorio* to deal with, but there was also the issue of originality, closely associated in the nineteenth century with the concept of genius, and the apparent clash of the solemn purpose of Bach's sacred music with its frivolous secular origins.

The complete edition of Bach's works begun in 1850 was forced to confront this in the preface to its 1856 edition of the *Christmas Oratorio*. The strategy of the work's editor, Wilhelm Rust, was to emphasize the role of chorales, which were both sacred and original to the composition, and to declare that the apparent secular origin of the music was essentially a red herring. Bach knew all along, Rust suggested, that the music he had composed for those secular occasions would find use in sacred works. Several problems disappeared with this assertion, because the notes became sacred by their nature, conceived that way from the start and remaining so whether used in a secular work or a sacred one. The originality problem was inherently solved, too, because this explanation let Bach off the hook; if he had been planning all along, then there was no lack of imaginative genius anywhere in the process. (This scenario is actually unlikely; its problems are discussed in chapter 4.)

There remained the fundamental problem of the *Christmas Oratorio*'s apparent lack of seriousness and weight compared with Bach's Passions, and for this there was an interpretive solution that dated from the earliest critical writings on the work in the 1840s. The most influential were by the musical antiquarian Carl von Winterfeld, who was evidently the first to recognize the parody origins of much of the *Oratorio* and to identify at least one of its secular models. Perhaps unsurprisingly for the leading historian of German church music, Winterfeld argued that Bach's use of certain chorale melodies deepened the theological seriousness of the *Christmas Oratorio*, in particular by drawing the work closer to his Passion settings.

Winterfeld's principal example is the first chorale harmonization in the work, "Wie soll ich dich empfangen?" The text is a verse of an Advent hymn that fittingly asks of Jesus, "How shall I receive you?"—a question well suited to the first part's theme of preparation for the nativity (the first aria instructs "Prepare yourself, Zion") (audio example 6.2) 🔊. Bach set this chorale stanza to a melody that students of his music will certainly recognize, but the way Winterfeld identified it was essential. He called the melody "O Haupt voll Blut und Wunden," familiar to many today in its English-language version "O sacred head now wounded." This text is closely associated with the Passion story and, indeed, is a chorale for Holy Week; it was part of a series of hymns that each reflected on a body part of Jesus.

This was Winterfeld's opening, and he charged through it, expressing wonder at the sounding of the notes of a Passion chorale in a Christmas oratorio. He claimed an analogy to sixteenth-century paintings (none identified specifically) that show the infant Jesus attended by both an angel of childhood and an angel of suffering and death. Just as those paintings supposedly foreshadow Jesus's crucifixion, so Bach was said to anticipate the Passion (and the *Passion*) by juxtaposing Christmas hymns such as "Gelobet seist du, Jesu Christ" and "Vom Himmel hoch, da komm ich her" (both heard in the *Christmas Oratorio*) with a chorale melody associated with the Passion story.

This interpretation accomplished several things. For one, it made Bach into a deep and serious thinker about the nature of Christmas. For another, it tempered the joyous exuberance of the *Christmas Oratorio* with something somber and presumably more fitting. And most important, it tied the *Christmas Oratorio*, with its suspect lightness and connections to secular music, firmly to Bach's Passions. This was particularly true because the *St. Matthew Passion*'s interpolated texts include no fewer than five verses of "O Haupt voll Blut und Wunden" and one verse of another hymn that uses the same melody; in many ways, this chorale tune stood for that Passion setting (audio example 6.3) 🔊. And of course, the *St. Matthew Passion* encapsulated everything that was valued about Bach.

This claim persists today—one runs across it again and again in popular and critical writings alike. There is just one problem: in eighteenth-century terms, it is almost certainly wrong. It is true that the melody Bach used for "Wie soll ich dich empfangen?" is today known as a Passion chorale; in fact, it is often called The Passion Chorale, as if there were only one. But this is a modern designation, which almost certainly comes from the very centrality of Bach's *St. Matthew Passion* in the repertory. One is likely to call the tune "O Haupt voll Blut und Wunden" precisely if the work you know best is the *St. Matthew Passion*. In Bach's time, the melody was used for numerous different texts for various seasons and tended to be identified as "Herzlich tut mich verlangen nach einem seel'gen End" (I long in my heart for a blessed end).

The *Christmas Oratorio* text "Wie soll ich dich empfangen?" is the first stanza of an Advent hymn. It was not in the Leipzig hymnal, but there was an option open to Bach in setting it to music. Because hymn poetry was regular and limited to a relatively small number of metrical patterns and stanza lengths, a hymn text could be sung to a variety of melodies. And in fact a 1736 hymnal published in Leipzig in which Bach had a hand suggests a tune for "Wie soll ich dich empfangen?": "Herzlich tut mich verlangen," the melody Bach indeed used in the *Christmas Oratorio*. But it is worth noting that the tune is not called "O Haupt voll Blut und Wunden" there, and that the hymnal also suggests the same tune for texts variously assigned to the evening, penitence, communion, Advent, the Passion, divine sovereignty and providence, temporal suffering, praise and thanks, death, and the feast of the Purification. Each time it is identified not as "O Haupt voll Blut und Wunden" (the Passion text) but as "Herzlich tut mich verlangen," a meditation on the believer's wish for death and eternal joy. To Leipzig listeners, this was not exclusively or even primarily a Passion melody.

Winterfeld made the same argument about the final chorale of part VI of the *Christmas Oratorio*, which uses the same tune, this time splendidly set with trumpets and drums. The text, "Nun seid ihr wohl gerochen," is a verse of the Christmas hymn "Ihr Christen auserkoren." (audio example 6.4) 🔊 Like the first chorale in the *Oratorio*, it was not in the regular Leipzig hymnal, and its own melody was probably not well known there. And as with the first chorale, Bach chose a tune that fit the meter—the same one as he used for "Wie soll ich dich empfangen?" Once again we are on shaky ground in claiming that his listeners would have heard a reference to the Passion. We need to recognize that this was an argument with a purpose, drawing the *Christmas Oratorio* closer to the Bach Passions with which it was implicitly and explicitly compared, and against which it had a hard time making a case for itself as a piece worthy of a devout composer.

Winterfelds's arguments establishing the gravitas of the *Christmas Oratorio* might well have played a role in the Sing-Akademie's decision to perform the work, and its complete performance, the first anywhere, took place in Berlin in 1857. (Note that Bach almost certainly never performed the whole himself, as discussed in chapter 5.) The organization had prepared some vocal parts as early as the 1830s but gave no public performance, and there is no documentation even of private rehearsal of the music. There had been partial performances in three other cities in the 1830s, '40s, and '50s, but the work was not part of the general repertory and had apparently not been heard since Bach's time.

The forces used in 1857 were very much like those the Sing-Akademie had been deploying since its 1829 performance of the *St. Matthew Passion*. The disposition started with the Sing-Akademie's purpose and amateur membership, which provided the chorus around which the performance was built musically and conceptually; instrumental players and trained soloists came from professional ranks. The ensemble for the *Christmas Oratorio* in 1857 consisted of a chorus of around two hundred, an orchestra of approximately fifty players, and professional soloists to sing the arias and other solo music. This mode of performance, different in size and conception from Bach's, was established by the Sing-Akademie and organizations like it as the norm for the performance of this kind of music and is responsible for the modern understanding of works such as the *Christmas Oratorio* and Bach's Passions as choral-orchestral-soloist music. This is a label (and a performing practice) they have never really escaped.

The Sing-Akademie's performance of the *Christmas Oratorio* took place among its presentations of other oratorio repertory, including the first complete performances of Bach's *Mass in B Minor* just a year before. Except for those *Mass* performances, Bach had been out of the Sing-Akademie's repertory since 1840, the year of its repeat performance of the *St. Matthew Passion*. Most of its fare consisted of new works (pieces by Mendelssohn and Robert Schumann among them), with fairly frequent performances of Handel's *Messiah*, which had not yet acquired its present-day association with Christmas.

The Sing-Akademie's complete performance was not so complete, though. It traversed all six parts of the *Oratorio* but cut seventeen numbers. A few of the eliminated movements were chorale settings (but not the Passion Chorale!), and one was a passage of gospel narrative, but most of the cuts were in solo music: eight of the work's thirteen arias and four of its ten instrumentally accompanied recitatives. This tips the balance in the work toward the gospel narrative and the framing choruses and chorales. It inverts the emphasis of the original, in which commentary in the form of poetic movements and chorales dominates.

It probably should not surprise that a choral organization would favor choral pieces, but the effect of the cuts was to tilt the work toward the powerful presentation of fully scored movements performed by large forces. The result resembled the cut-down versions of the *St. Matthew Passion* presented by the Sing-Akademie; those performances also eliminated most of that work's arias, and the overall effect was dominated by movements such as the opening chorus. The elimination of so many of the *Christmas Oratorio*'s arias tempered problematic aspects like poetic texts and movements that called for solo vocal virtuosity. The various strategies that brought the *Christmas Oratorio* closer to Bach's Passions succeeded, but they established a particular perspective of the work that is still influential today.

The first critical engagement with the *Christmas Oratorio*, its publication, and its earliest modern performances all took place within a few years in the middle of the nineteenth century, closely tied to the reception of Bach's Passions and very much concerned with the work's genesis. Little on the *Oratorio* that was new appeared until a 1916 article in the *Neue Zeitschrift für Musik*, which claimed that two of its gospel choruses originated in older music, just like the poetic arias and choruses. This assertion proposed to extend the parody origins of the *Christmas Oratorio* beyond its concerted poetic numbers into its gospel setting. The claim, now one hundred years old, has hung on despite a lack of evidence, and it turns out to have a dark side, tied up in stereotypes of Jews and their musical depiction. Parody turned out to be an open-ended outlet for interpretations of Bach's music that were both dubious and distasteful. Strikingly, this aspect of the reception of the *Christmas Oratorio* is also closely connected to his Passion music, and in this it fits with other aspects of the work's reception.

The article's author, Gerhard Freiesleben, claimed that Bach's setting of the words of the wise men in part V that begin "Wo ist der neugeborne König der Juden?" (Where is the newborn king of the Jews?) and, after an interpolated poetic text set as a recitative, continue

"Wir haben seinen Stern gesehen" (We have seen his star) had been adapted from his lost *St. Mark Passion* BWV 247, in particular from the gospel chorus "Pfui dich, wie fein zerbrichst du den Tempel," which narrates the mocking of Jesus on the cross by passersby (audio examples 6.5a and 6.5b) 🔊.

Freiesleben was probably set down this path by the peculiar status of the *St. Mark Passion*. Its complete libretto is known, and even though no musical sources survive, some of the score has long been regarded as within reach. Many of the *Passion*'s numerous chorales are probably transmitted in collections of Bach's four-part settings. Some of its solo and tutti arias were clearly planned as parodies, particularly of movements from the so-called *Ode of Mourning* BWV 198 that Bach had composed for a royal-electoral memorial service in 1729 and that survives (audio examples 6.6a and 6.6b) 🔊. Within limits, these concerted numbers can be recovered to some degree, though with questions about key, instrumentation, recomposition of vocal lines to accommodate new texts, and even whether planned parodies were actually carried out.

The lost gospel narrative is another matter and evidently became an irresistible challenge, particularly for those for whom Passion settings stand at the center of Bach's output. These feelings have arguably contributed to the zeal with which people have attempted to "reconstruct" the *St. Mark Passion* in many different ways, seeking to salve the wound that the loss represents. (This topic is discussed in detail in my earlier book, *Hearing Bach's Passions*. See Suggestions for Further Reading and Listening.)

Freiesleben's kind of argument—that a known work originated in a lost model—depends on two things: the suggestion that we should suspect parody in the first place from characteristics (particularly defects) of an extant piece, and the claim that a reconstructed hypothetical older version of a work itself makes musical and textual sense, perhaps even better sense than the supposedly derived version. Having found fault with the *Christmas Oratorio* movement (we will return to his objections in a moment), Freiesleben proposed an earlier version bearing the *St. Mark* text and defended it as likely, appealing to pictorial and text-expressive features of the reconstructed model and claiming its "natural" character, a strategy by which the supposed original version was claimed to be better than the surviving one. He printed a "reconstruction" of the lost *St. Mark* chorus using the music of the *Christmas Oratorio,* though he was forced to make many adjustments to accommodate the *Passion* text. He justified this by claiming that such modifications were typical of the parody process. He was arguing both ways: the music fits the new text perfectly (which it doesn't, in fact), and places where it doesn't fit are entirely normal.

Even the character of the autograph score, clearly in Bach's working script rather than the fair-copy hand typically found in parodies, is explained away as the product of the many revisions that might have been necessary in making the supposed parody. In other words, it's a parody because it looks on the page like a new composition.

We can probably understand the lengths to which Freiesleben was willing to go in light of the article's telling last sentence: "And so we can consider ourselves convinced, without objection, that here a heretofore unrecognized fragment of the *St. Mark Passion* has again come to light." The essay's title promises "A new contribution to the history of the *Christmas Oratorio*'s genesis," but this last sentence reveals its true aim: the recovery of music from the *St. Mark Passion*. If you know the history of ardent and quixotic searches for the lost *St. Mark Passion*, you should probably be immediately suspicious of this claim about the *Christmas Oratorio*.

Even more striking is the other half of the author's argument, the basis of his suspicion of this *Christmas Oratorio* chorus in the first place. He wrote that "the manner of Bach's composition [in setting the text 'Where is the newborn king of the Jews?'] agrees neither with the worthy station of kings nor with the detached calm of wise men, informed by the star and going to worship the new kingly son. They would not storm into a royal palace with the baying call 'Wo—wo, wo,' would not cut each other off in the manner of 'wir haben seinen Stern gesehen' as if they wanted to shout each other down." This extraordinary passage takes a typical approach—it finds problems with a Bach text setting and explains them by parody—but the principal objection here is aesthetic. This is said to be a setting unbefitting Bach or the context, pictorially inappropriate measured against certain dramatic ideals.

Those ideals are Mendelssohn's, because Freiesleben compared this supposedly deficient music with "the wondrous setting of the same passage in Mendelssohn's *Christus* fragment" and found "something amiss." The piece to which Freiesleben referred is from a project that spanned some ten years and was left unfinished at Mendelssohn's death: a three-part oratorio with the working title *Erde, Hölle und Himmel* (Earth, Hell, and Heaven). The surviving portions (probably from the Earth section) consist of texts narrating Jesus's birth and a Passion section strongly influenced by Bach's works. The title *Christus* under which the fragments were published suggests a kind of combined Christmas oratorio and Passion but was probably never used by the composer. It is how Freiesleben knew the piece, though, and the opening text of the surviving fragment happens to correspond exactly to the narrative portion of part V of Bach's *Christmas Oratorio*, beginning with "Da Jesus geboren war zu Bethlehem" (When Jesus was born in Bethlehem). The movement Freiesleben cited—Mendelssohn's setting of the text "Wo ist der neugeborne König der Juden?"—is a model of consonance, lyricism, textural subtlety, and vocal order (audio example 6.7).

It is complicated indeed for Freiesleben to have invoked Mendelssohn, a converted Jew who was nonetheless the object of anti-Semitic disdain, of all people, as the composer who shows the proper Christian reverence in setting this New Testament narrative. But even leaving that issue aside, Freiesleben's reasoning (if that is the right word) was obviously problematic as a guide to the parody origin of this music from the *Christmas Oratorio*. To criticize the work in this way was to acknowledge it as fundamentally flawed and beneath Bach.

But there is more here, because Freiesleben's language was unmistakable in its tone and diction. In speaking of "storming," a "baying call," shouting over one another, and generally inappropriate vocal behavior, Freiesleben invoked the acoustic stereotype of the Jew. The passage cites cacophony, noise, and disorder, exactly the sounds most closely associated with Jews. (One does not need to look beyond Richard Wagner's infamous essay *Das Judenthum in der Musik*, first published in 1850, to find parallel characterizations of Jewish speech and music, and of course, this idea goes back much further.) In Freiesleben's view, this *Christmas Oratorio* chorus is a parody because it is in the voice of gentile kings but sounds like Jews. His objection thus might not have been aesthetic but rather a matter of fundamental discomfort with the idea that figures in the narrative who recognize the divinity of Jesus are represented in this way.

Freiesleben not only found problems with the *Christmas Oratorio* chorus by reference to the acoustic stereotype of Jews, but also identified a likely parody model in the same way. The passage evidently reminded him of music from Bach's Passions, so he suggested that the lost *St. Mark Passion* was the place to look, claiming that "there is one among them whose text can be underlaid word for word without the slightest difficulty in our choral movement. It is the first chorus of the Jews before the cross and reads: 'Pfui dich, wie fein zerbrichest du den Tempel.'" Freiesleben took for granted that there is such a thing as a "chorus of Jews" associated with a particular compositional technique.

The claim that the text from Mark can be underlaid "without the slightest difficulty" is false; Freiesleben himself provided multiple alternatives in his attempt at "reconstruction."

The idea that the musical style of the movement somehow points to a chorus of Jews and that the music from the *Christmas Oratorio* belongs with these words is all the more loaded because of Martin Luther's translation of this passage. The opening words of the Passion text from Mark's gospel, "Pfui dich," typically rendered "Ah" or "Aha" in most English versions, following the Greek, are connected with the German word for spitting. (There is a German expression of disdain, "Pfui Teufel," associated with superstitious spitting and a likely connection with the Yiddish interjection "Feh.") This expression was presumably meant to resonate with the gospels' description of Jesus being spat on, a loaded text by any measure and an ugly phrase for Luther to have ascribed to anyone. Freiesleben's selection of it as a characteristic "chorus of Jews" was especially fraught.

Who was this author? Gerhard Julius Freiesleben was born in 1880 and was the son of a prominent Leipzig jurist. He was educated at the St. Thomas School and Leipzig University, graduating in law with a 1906 dissertation on the legal status of corporate officers. He practiced law in Leipzig and was the author of a book for nonspecialists on the legal rights of musical authors and publishers. Freiesleben had musical interests and training and published several articles in music journals, mostly on legal topics. One article is on the justifications for time limits for copyright; this is noteworthy because of Freiesleben's role in the attempt to pass a so-called *Lex Parsifal*. At issue was the expiration of copyright protection on older works; a group of interested parties (led by Wagner's heirs) campaigned to make a legal exception for *Parsifal* to help limit its production to Wagner's own theater in Bayreuth. A failed attempt to protect all of Wagner's works in 1901 was followed by one around 1912 aimed specifically at *Parsifal* and involving a petition signed by eighteen thousand "German citizens." Freiesleben is cited as chair of the Leipzig faction advocating for the law, and he wrote to Hans von Wolzogen, a prominent Wagnerite, with strategic advice about the campaign, fearing that "the Jewish press" would seize on details to accuse the Bayreuth leadership of being behind the effort (which, in fact, they were). Freiesleben's professional interests and expertise touched directly on this musical and political matter.

Freiesleben published one other article on a Bach subject, a three-part piece that appeared a year after his *Christmas Oratorio* essay. Its title is "On the Performance of Bach's Large Choral Works," and its starting point is the claim that the modern listener cannot be expected to sit through a three- or four-hour sacred concert performance. (This, it should be noted, came from an advocate for Wagner's music dramas.) The large Bach works thus need to be shortened. Freiesleben argued that the real goal in shortening the *Christmas Oratorio*, never intended to be performed at a stretch, was to make it into a true oratorio. His models were, of course, Bach's Passion settings, so his exercise in abridgment sought, at least in part, to make the *Christmas Oratorio* more like the Passions. He further asserted that the "lyrical and contemplative" *Christmas Oratorio* cannot captivate the listener the way the "sublime and tragic" Passions can. Here we see the continuing tendency to judge and interpret the *Christmas Oratorio* in the context of Bach's Passion settings. In Freiesleben's case, this tendency extends further than usual in his earlier article's assertion that some of the Christmas music was indeed from a Passion.

Freiesleben's poorly argued, implausible, and racist essay could easily be dismissed if it had not been so influential. Its result must have been doubly appealing, seeming to solve a mystery of the *Christmas Oratorio* and to recover bits of the *St. Mark Passion*. Two authors writing after World War II independently picked up its conclusions and—in somewhat less explicit but still recognizable form—some of its aesthetic foundations as well. One, writing in 1968, essentially appropriated the results, confusingly arguing that Freiesleben's arguments were wrong but his results correct; the author quoted Freiesleben's 1916 article selectively, leaving out the explicit reference to Jews but including all the loaded words. He then took a next step, proposing another *Christmas Oratorio* chorus ("Lasset uns nun gehen gen Bethlehem" [Let us now go to Bethlehem]) as derived from another lost *St. Mark* chorus. Jews weren't mentioned, but blithering, demagoguery, vehemence, and obstinacy were—all classic stereotypes of Jews and their speech. You can probably guess how this article ended: "And so in the second turba chorus of the *Christmas Oratorio* we have doubtless rediscovered a further turba chorus from the *St. Mark Passion*." The attraction of the *St. Mark Passion* continued.

Another author, writing in 1978, was at least straightforward about his principal interest in recovering the *St. Mark Passion*. This writer accepted Freiesleben's conclusions "without doubt," then asked, "If there is one use of parody in the *Christmas Oratorio*, why not two or three?" He, too, turned his attention to "Lasset uns nun gehen gen Bethlehem" and found it likely that there was also a model for that piece, turning inevitably to the lost *St. Mark Passion*. He settled on a particular chorus from the *Passion* as its supposed model, but it is telling that he did not know the 1968 author's work and identified a different *Passion* chorus as the sure model for the same *Christmas Oratorio* movement. (Keep in mind that the music of the "model" does not survive; all this consists of guesses based on the text of the lost *Passion*. The rules of this game are so loose that it is possible to make almost any text fit any music, and one quickly realizes that the assertions did not come close to being arguments made from evidence.)

Perhaps the strangest claim of all in this study was that the *Christmas Oratorio*'s "Ehre sei Gott in der Höhe, und Friede auf Erden, und dem Menschen ein Wohlgefallen" (Glory to God in the highest, and peace on earth, and goodwill towards humankind) was derived from the lost *Passion*'s two "Kreuzige ihn" (Crucify him) choruses. This took some doing, given that the texts are affectively so different. The argument was flimsy but characteristic of a certain kind of Bach interpretation—and a reminder of the shadow of Passion music that lurks over the Christmas work. The author asserted that both texts ("Glory to God" and "Crucify him") are about "elevation" in different ways—glorification in the nativity chorus of angels and Jesus's high place on the cross in the passage from the Passion narrative. There was a musical claim, too: the melodic interval that opens "Ehre sei Gott in der Höhe" (and thus the "Crucify him" choruses, in this theory), known as a "fourth," was said to be found in Bach's Passions and cantatas, where it supposedly invokes the cross because of the crosslike graphical shape of the numeral 4.

Do not bother looking in the Suggestions for Further Reading and Listening at the back of this book for literature on this point; it is entirely made up, as far as I can tell, and represents the sort of ad hoc pseudo-theological argument encountered frequently in some kinds of Bach interpretation, combined with a love for the arcane and mystical symbolism some people hope to find in Bach. If this theory about "Ehre sei Gott in der Höhe" has gained traction—which it has—it is probably because it resonates with a tendency for commentators to link the *Christmas Oratorio* to Passion settings whenever possible.

Some of this speculation has stuck; it is difficult today to find a treatment of the *Christmas Oratorio* that does not mention at least the possibility that its gospel choruses were adapted from the *St. Mark Passion*. I find the claims implausible on musical and source-critical grounds, but more important, it is clear that they originate in some disturbing ideologies. And even though the most obviously racist language of Freiesleben's original article is gone, its ideas and code words remain, both in discussions of this topic and in treatments of Bach's oratorios in general. A recent theological interpretation of the *St. John Passion*, for example, describes the "Jesum von Nazareth" choruses sung "as the crowd clamours" for Jesus, this way: "In this movement, the chorus follows the oboes, second violin and viola in a cackle of strings and woodwind. This produces a tumultuous babble of voices, all shouting over each other, while the woodwind mocks Jesus." "Tumultuous babble," "cackle," and "shouting over each other"—this language could be straight out of the 1916 article.

Alas, Freiesleben's explicit invocations of Jewish stereotypes, which launched so much speculation about the *Christmas Oratorio*, are not the extent of the problem, nor even are studies that take his dubious results as a starting point. I think there is a bigger issue here, because these theories intersect with a modern performance ideal of gospel choral passages in Bach's narrative works, particularly those representing Jews or loosely identified as "crowds," as loud, fast, and vehement. It is not news that this element of Bach performance is the source of many of the difficult questions about anti-Jewish sentiment in these works, but it is now evident that scholarship was led down essentially the same path.

And this brings us back to the music of the *Christmas Oratorio*. Its gospel narrative consists mostly of words of the evangelist but does include some direct speech: of an angel, of the heavenly hosts, of shepherds, of the wise men, and of Herod. The speech of individuals is presented by individual singers, that of groups by the combined voices of the principal singers forming the chorus. This is, of course, the same model as in Bach's Passions, and many questionable ideas about the Passion settings contributed to the desire to find Passion parodies in the *Christmas Oratorio*'s music in the first place. For example, one of the interpretive problem of the Passions has been a tendency to speak loosely about the musical depiction of "crowds" in the narrative, a term (as in "crowd chorus") that carries with it ugly ideas about a mob often casually identified as Jewish. But, as has been repeatedly pointed out, John's gospel never refers to a "crowd," and the groups Bach musically represents in both surviving Passion settings have particular identities—disciples, soldiers, passersby, and so on (and, in fact, sometimes "the Jews").

The habit of referring generically to "crowd choruses" and of finding some kind of aesthetic satisfaction in loud, fast, and vehement performance of them by large modern choral ensembles almost certainly has affected the way people have heard and thought about the

Christmas Oratorio. I suspect this was a starting point for Freiesleben; the *Oratorio*'s "Wo—wo—wo ist der neugeborne König der Juden?" probably sounded too much like "Wir—wir—wir haben keinen König denn den Keiser" (We have no king but Caesar") from the *St. John Passion* for him to ignore (audio examples 6.8a and 6.8b) 🔊.

But it took a particular view of what a "crowd chorus" should sound like in a performance by large forces for him to imagine he heard a Passion movement behind the words of the wise men in the Christmas work. This view effectively makes "Wo ist der neugeborne König der Juden?" a crowd chorus, even in its original context. It requires a regard for the *Christmas Oratorio* as some kind of lesser relative of the Passions to hear the music that way; the connection would not have been possible without this view, established in the first years of the *Oratorio*'s modern reception.

The oddest case of all is the chorus "Ehre sei Gott in der Höhe," in some ways the most extraordinary piece in the entire *Christmas Oratorio*. Strictly speaking, it presents the words of the heavenly hosts singing "Glory to God," but of course, it is more. These are the words that open the Gloria of the Mass Ordinary, and they were intimately linked to the musical observation of Christmas in central Germany, because there was a long tradition of settings of this text as a motet for the season. Even smaller musical establishments could present such a piece, because a motet was for voices (and continuo) only, in contrast to concerted settings with instruments. German motet style, used for biblical passages and chorales or both together, was a relative of the antique musical style inherited from the generation of Giovanni Pierluigi da Palestrina (and discussed in detail in chapter 3).

Collections of motets from the early eighteenth century from Thuringia and other parts of central Germany include more settings of "Ehre sei Gott in der Höhe" than of any other text; this was a musical Christmas tradition. Bach responds in the *Christmas Oratorio* with a motet setting of the text but one that finds roles for instruments while still keeping to the musical characteristics associated with the motet. First, the movement is organized in the manner of a motet, treating each of the three phrases of the text ("Ehre sei Gott in der Höhe / und Friede auf Erden / und dem Menschen ein Wohlgefallen") in distinct musical units. Each is presented separately and reaches a strong musical arrival before the next is taken up (audio examples 6.9a–6.9c) 🔊.

In keeping with one of the musical traditions of the motet, the two outer sections are imitative, with successive entrances of the voices with the same musical idea and the combination of the independent voices in counterpoint as the basis of the music. This is hidden at the opening; Bach has three of the voices enter at once, presumably for the striking effect of their sudden appearance. Each presents filler material until its turn to sing the imitative opening subject, so one does not hear their successive entrances with the subject very clearly.

The other nod to the motet genre is the way instruments are used. Bach employs all the strings and woodwind instruments but in a very particular fashion. Instruments often participated in German motets but not independently; they doubled the vocal lines, playing along exactly with the voices. This was the essential difference between a motet and a vocal concerto (the kind of piece represented by the choruses and arias in the *Christmas Oratorio* and most of Bach's other vocal instrumental music). In "Ehre sei Gott in der Höhe," Bach finds ways to incorporate the instruments that stay just within the bounds of the motet.

In the first section ("Ehre sei Gott"), all the instruments play a transparent chordal accompaniment that provides harmonic support for the voices but offers no melodic competition with them. In the second section ("und Friede auf Erden"), the strings and flutes are given a rhythmically regular, harmonically conceived three-note accompanimental figure; this is not meant to draw melodic attention but, in fact, resembles the kind of motivic accompaniment occasionally found in motets. In this section, the four oboes play in long, slow-moving notes; their material is purely harmonic, supporting the rest of the ensemble. And in the third section, "und dem Menschen ein wohlgefallen," the oboes continue this role, while the strings and flutes do precisely what one expects in a motet: they double the imitative voices.

The stylistic background of this chorus is relevant here because it allows us to see how well the movement fits in the *Christmas Oratorio*. We do not need to explain it as music adapted from a Passion setting, and Bach's autograph score makes it clear that this was an original composition, not the adaptation of an older movement. But a listener cannot hear that; he or she can hear only that the movement has deep stylistic connections to music relevant to the time, place, and season.

At this point, you should have an objection. Perhaps Bach did adapt this from a Passion setting, transforming it affectively from the context of a chorus calling for Jesus's crucifixion to the joyful outburst of the heavenly hosts. This would have been no more extreme than the transformation of "Bereite dich, Zion" from its rage aria model (discussed in chapter 4). But there is an essential difference here: the very suggestion of a parody in the first place came from the proposer's assertion that there were things wrong with the *Christmas Oratorio* chorus: That it did not resemble Bach's "usual" settings of this text (or the Latin "Gloria in excelsis"), although it is never specified what that is; that it does not begin with the expected imitation (a claim both prescriptive and false, once you understand how and why Bach has masked the opening imitation); and that the movement is dramatically unjustified (an essentially meaningless comment and certainly one that pays no attention to the pervasive repertory of "Ehre sei Gott" motets). Add the incorrect claims about the nature of Bach's autograph and the wholly invented symbolism of the number 4, and the entire premise collapses. Yes, any movement could be a parody, but it takes a particular view of the *Christmas Oratorio* and its relationship to Passion music to motivate and defend a claim that a good movement in the Christmas work must owe its origin to a Passion setting.

    The interpretation of the *Christmas Oratorio* has continued to be influenced most of all by that 1829 performance of the *St. Matthew Passion*, which set the tone for the reception of Bach's sacred music. We are, I think, capable of stepping outside that view. The question posed in the *Christmas Oratorio*'s first chorale—"How shall I receive you?"—is worth asking about the work itself, and the answer does not have to include Bach's Passion settings as our first point of engagement with this matchless music.

Epilogue: How to Listen to Bach

There is, of course, no one way to listen to Bach. People listen in every conceivable manner, and there is no basis for saying that one way is better than any other. But there are ways of listening to Bach that might not have occurred to you, including those that take eighteenth-century musical sensibilities into account or that recognize the consequences of our place as listeners in the twenty-first century and as inheritors of a long performing tradition. The aim of this book has been to suggest and encourage those ways of listening.

An awareness of musical style as it was understood in the eighteenth century might be the most important tool for doing this. With it, you can listen to almost any piece of sacred or liturgical music of the time and recognize where it stands on the spectrum of old and new styles. You can learn to understand the musical constructive techniques that go along with each of these styles and start to grasp the choices composers made and the ways they exploited various styles and even their combination. This, in turn, opens the possibility of listening to what compositions might be saying in musical terms, even aside from text expression, theological meaning, or other aspects that are fundamentally about words rather than notes.

An awareness of musical style can help you hear what is musically most characteristic of movements in eighteenth-century terms, including the markers of types such as sleep arias, love duets, secular choral arias, and so on. This can give you musical starting points for understanding how Bach and his librettists used these types in the *Mass in B Minor* and the *Christmas Oratorio*.

And a sensitivity to style and musical construction can give you ways to listen to and think about music that is often first discussed in terms of its parody relationship to older music. As I have argued, parody origin, though interesting, is not audible most of the time and is of little consequence compared with what a piece tells you by its musical style and construction. At the least, an appreciation of the settings themselves (and not just their largely inaudible prehistory) will let you steer clear of the genetic fallacy and its dubious shortcut path that suggests that a movement's origins explains what is interesting about it. If you came to this book already liking the *Mass in B Minor*, my guess is that you appreciate the work for how it sounds, not because of its origins. There is plenty to learn about that musical sound—and more to listen to.

The other insight you can bring to your listening to this music concerns our place in the twenty-first century. When we make choices about how to perform Bach's compositions, we stamp the result with our ideas about this music. There is no right way to perform it but no wrong way, either, and certainly no neutral way that makes no choices, decisions, or impositions on the received musical text. You can learn to listen for those choices, whether in a performance that most values historical perspectives or one that adopts aspects of this music's reception since the nineteenth century.

Your skills as a listener can help you hear aspects of the modern performance of Bach's music that are the product of its reception and interpretation over the last 150 years, ways in which ideas about this music's meanings influence its performance today. We have more access to this repertory now than at any other time in history, and we can listen in new ways every time we return to it. That's an enormous luxury, and you can take full advantage by learning some new—and old—ways of listening.

Appendix: Tables

Table 1.1. The sections of J. S. Bach's autograph score of the *Mass in B Minor*

	Contents	Origin of the manuscript
No. 1 Missa	Kyrie and Gloria	Score from 1733
No. 2 Symbolum Nicenum	Credo	Newly composed/assembled in 1749
No. 3 Sanctus	Sanctus	From 1724, newly recopied in 1749
No. 4 Osanna, Benedictus, Agnus Dei, et Dona nobis pacem	[remainder]	Newly composed/assembled in 1749

Table 2.1. Reuse and parody in the *Mass in B Minor*

	Model or movements that share music	
Kyrie eleison I	*Likely parody; model unknown*	
Christe eleison	*Likely parody; model unknown*	
Kyrie eleison II	*Likely parody; model unknown*	
Gloria in excelsis Deo	*Likely parody; model unknown*	
Et in terra pax	*Likely parody; model unknown*	
Laudamus te	*Likely parody; model unknown*	
Gratias agimus tibi	"Wir danken dir, Gott, wir danken dir" BWV 29/2	= BWV 232^I (1733 Missa for Dresden)
Domine Deus/Domini Fili	*Likely parody; model unknown*	
Qui tollis peccata mundi	"Schauet doch und sehet" BWV 46/1	
Qui sedes ad dextram Patris	*Likely parody; model unknown*	
Quoniam tu solus sanctus	*Likely parody; model unknown*	
Cum Sancto Spiritu	*Likely parody; model unknown*	
Credo in unum Deum	= Credo in G major BWV deest	
Patrem omnipotentem	"Gott, wie dein Name, so ist auch dein Ruhm" BWV 171/1 and earlier work [lost]	
Et in unum Dominum	*Likely parody; model unknown*	
Et incarnatus est	**Newly composed**	
Crucifixus	"Weinen, Klagen, Sorgen, Zagen" BWV 12/2	
Et resurrexit	Possibly "Entfernet euch, ihr heitern Sterne" BWV Anh. I 9/1 [lost]	
Et in Spiritum Sanctum	*Likely parody; model unknown*	
Confiteor	**Newly composed**	
Et expecto resurrectionem	"Jauchzet, ihr erfreuten Stimmen" BWV 120/2 and "Herr Gott, Beherrscher alle Dinge" BWV 120a/1 and "Zahle, Zion, die Gelübde" BWV 120b/2	
Sanctus	= Sanctus BWV deest	
Osanna in excelsis	"Preise dein Glücke" BWV 215/1 and "Es lebe der König" BWV Anh. 11/1 [lost]	
Benedictus	*Likely parody; model unknown*	
Agnus Dei	"Ach, bleibe doch, mein liebstes Leben" BWV 11/4 and "Entfernet euch, ihr kalten Herzen" BWV Anh. 14/3 [lost]	
Dona nobis pacem	"Wir danken dir, Gott, wir danken dir" BWV 29/2 and "Gratias agimus tibi" BWV 232^I/7	

Table 3.1. Movements of the *Mass in B Minor* sorted by style

Old style	Old style with instrumental "voices"	Mixed old and modern elements	Modern style with vocal imitation	Modern style
3. Kyrie eleison II	13. Credo in unum Deum	7. Gratias agimus tibi	1. Kyrie eleison I	Ritornello movements
20. Confiteor		27. Dona nobis pacem	5. Et in terra pax	2. Christe eleison
			12. Cum sancto spiritu	4. Gloria in excelsis Deo
			22b. Pleni sunt coeli	6. Laudamus te
				8. Domine Deus/Domini Fili
				9. Qui tollis peccata mundi
				10. Qui sedes ad dextram Patris
				11. Quoniam tu solus sanctus
				15. Et in unum Dominum
				18. Et resurrexit
				19. Et in Spiritum Sanctum
				21. Et expecto resurrectionem
				23/25. Osanna in excelsis
				24. Benedictus
				26. Agnus Dei
				Others
				14. Patrem omnipotentem
				16. Et incarnatus est
				17. Crucifixus
				22a. Sanctus

Table 4.1. Parody in the *Christmas Oratorio*

Model compositions—poetic movements	Christmas Oratorio—arias and selected recitatives

"Tönet, ihr Pauken!" BWV 214

Parts I–IV

1. Chorus: Tönet, ihr Pauken ⟶ 1. Chorus: Jauchzet, frohlocket
3. *Aria S: Blast die wohlgeriffnen Flöten* ⟶ 4. Aria A: Bereite dich, Zion
5. Aria A: Fromme Musen! meine Glieder ⟶ 8. Aria B: Grosser Herr, o starker König
7. Aria B: Kron und Preis gekrönter Damen ⟶ 15. Aria T: Frohe Hirten, eilt, ach eilet
9. Chorus: Blühet, ihr Linden in Sachsen, wie Zedern ⟶ 19. Aria A: Schlafe, mein Liebster

24. Chorus: Herrscher des Himmels, erhöre das Lallen

"Lasst uns sorgen, lasst uns wachen" BWV 213

29. Aria S/B: Herr, dein Mitleid
1. Chorus: Lasst uns sorgen, lasst uns wachen ⟶ **31. Aria A: Schliesse, mein Herze, dies selige Wunder**
3. Aria S: Schlafe, mein Liebster, und pflege der Ruh ⟶ 36. Chorus: Fallt mit Danken, fallt mit Loben
5. Aria A: Treues Echo dieser Orten ⟶ 39. Aria S: Flösst, mein Heiland
7. Aria T: Auf meinen Flügeln sollst du schweben ⟶ 41. Aria T: Ich will nur dir zu Ehren leben
9. Aria A: Ich will dich nicht hören, ich will dich nicht wissen
11. Aria A/T: Ich bin deine/Du bist meine
13. Chorus: Lust der Völker, Lust der Deinen

Parts V–VI

"Preise dein Glücke, gesegnetes Sachsen" BWV 215

43. Chorus: Ehre sei dir, Gott, gesungen
7. Aria S: Durch die von Eifer entflammten Waffen ⟶ 47. Aria B: Erleucht auch meine finstre Sinnen

Lost secular model	Intermediate church cantata
Chorus	Chorus
Recit.	Recit.
Aria	Aria
Recit	Recit.
Aria	Aria
Recit	Recit.
Aria	Aria
Recit	Recit.
	Chorale

51. Aria S/A/T: Ach, wenn wird die Zeit erscheinen?
52. Recit. A: Mein Liebester herrschet schon
54. Chorus: Herr, wenn die stolzen Feinde schnauben
56. Recit. S: Du Falscher, such nur den Herrn zu fällen
57. Aria S: Nur ein Wink von seinen Händen
61. Recit. T: So geht! Genug, mein Schatz
62. Aria T: Nun mögt ihr stolzen Feinde schrecken
63. Recit. S/A/T/B: Was will der Höllen Schrecken nun
64. Chorale: Nun seid ihr wohlgerochen

Movement in italics is not used in the *Christmas Oratorio*

Movements in boldface are new compositions

Table 4.2. The use of opening and closing model movements in the *Christmas Oratorio*

Model compositions—opening and closing choruses	Christmas Oratorio—opening choruses
<u>BWV 214</u> 1. Chorus: Tönet, ihr Pauken . . . 9. Chorus: Blühet, ihr Linden in Sachsen, wie Zedern	Part I 1. Chorus: Jauchzet, frohlocket Part II [no opening chorus]
<u>BWV 213</u> 1. Chorus: Lasst uns sorgen, lasst uns wachen . . . 13. Chorus: Lust der Völker, Lust der Deinen	Part III 24. Chorus: Herrscher des Himmels, erhöre das Lallen Part IV 36. Chorus: Fallt mit Danken, fallt mit Loben
[Lost model] [1. Opening chorus?]	Part V 43. Chorus: Ehre sei dir, Gott, gesungen Part VI 54. Chorus: Herr, wenn die stolzen Feinde schnauben

Appendix

Table 5.1. Bach's church cantatas performed in Leipzig in the Christmas season

Liturgical Year	Christmas Day	2nd Day	3rd Day	Sunday after Christmas*	New Year's Day	Sunday after New Year's	Epiphany
1723–24	BWV 63 (tpts/drums)	BWV 40 (horns)	BWV 64	—	BWV 190 (tpts/drums)	BWV 153	BWV 65 (horns)
1724–25	BWV 91 (horns/drums)	BWV 121	BWV 133	BWV 122	BWV 41 (tpts/drums)	—	BWV 123
1725–26	BWV 110 (tpts/drums)	BWV 57	BWV 151	BWV 28	BWV 16	—	?
[later]					BWV 171 (tpts/drums)		

*This feast does not figure in the *Christmas Oratorio*.

Table 5.2. The *Christmas Oratorio* at St. Thomas and St. Nicholas Churches in 1734–35

Feast	Date	Part	St. Nicholas	St. Thomas
Christmas Day	Saturday, December 25	I	morning	afternoon
2nd Day	Sunday, December 26	II	afternoon	morning
3rd Day	Monday, December 27	III	morning	——
New Year's Day	Saturday, January 1	IV	afternoon	morning
Sunday after New Year's	Sunday, January 2	V	morning	——
Epiphany	Thursday, January 6	VI	afternoon	morning

Table 5.3. Christmas season liturgical calendars, 1734–1750

Liturgical Year	Christmas Day		Matches 1734–35?
1734–35	Saturday		[first performance of the *Christmas Oratorio*]
1735–36	Sunday		N
1736–37	Tuesday		N
1737–38	Wednesday		N
1738–39	Thursday		N
1739–40	**Friday**	**Y**	
1740–41	Sunday		N
1741–42	Monday		N
1742–43	Tuesday		N
1743–44	Wednesday		N
1744–45	**Friday**	**Y**	
1745–46	**Saturday**	**Y**	
1746–47	Sunday		N
1747–48	Monday		N
1748–49	Wednesday		N
1749–50	Thursday		N

Table 5.4. Gospel text in the parts of the *Christmas Oratorio*

Part	Liturgical date	Gospel	BWV 248
I	Christmas Day	Lk 2:1–14 (birth, shepherds, angels)	Lk 2:1, 3–7 (birth)
II	2nd Day	Lk 2:15–20 (shepherds)	Lk 2:8–14 (shepherds, angels)
III	3rd Day	Jn 1:1–14 (prophecy)]	Lk 2:15–20 (shepherds)
IV	New Year's Day	Lk 2:21 (circumcision, naming)	Lk 2:21 (circumcision, naming)
V	Sunday after New Year's	Mt 2:13–23 (flight into Egypt)	Mt 2:1–6 (Herod)
VI	Epiphany	Mt 2:1–12 (Herod, wise men)	Mt 2:7–12 (wise men)

Suggestions for Further Reading and Listening

The suggestions offered here for further reading emphasize accessible writings in English. Citations are to the most recent and most widely available editions, not necessarily the earliest. I have generally not cited all the scholarly literature behind each of the discussions here. For complete citations to the literature on individual works and to more technical writings, consult the entries in Wolfgang Schmieder, *Thematisch-systematisches Verzeichnis der musikalischen Werke von Johann Sebastian Bach: Bach-Werke-Verzeichnis (BWV)* (Wiesbaden: Breitkopf & Härtel, 1950; 2nd ed., 1990; "small" ed., 1998); Hans-Joachim Schulze and Christoph Wolff, *Bach Compendium: Analytisch-bibliographisches Repertorium der Werke Johann Sebastian Bachs (BC)* (Leipzig and Frankfurt, 1985–); and the reference tools cited below.

General Literature on Bach

The enormous scholarly literature on Johann Sebastian Bach is accessible through reference works. A comprehensive guide to the literature (and to many issues in Bach studies) is Daniel R. Melamed and Michael Marissen, *An Introduction to Bach Studies* (New York: Oxford University Press, 1998). An excellent online guide to Bach reference materials by Stephen A. Crist is available on Oxford Bibliographies Online (www.oxfordbibliographies.com). There are good short articles on almost every topic in Malcolm Boyd and John Butt, eds., *Oxford Composer Companions: J. S. Bach* (Oxford and New York: Oxford University Press, 1999).

Of the many biographies of Bach (surveyed in Melamed and Marissen, *An Introduction to Bach Studies*), two accessible short studies in English are Malcolm Boyd, *Bach*, 3rd ed. (Oxford: Oxford University Press, 2000); and the entry on Johann Sebastian in Christoph Wolff et al., *The New Grove Bach Family* (New York: W. W. Norton, 1997), and on Grove Music Online (www.oxfordmusiconline.com). The most up-to-date longer work is Christoph Wolff, *Johann Sebastian Bach: The Learned Musician* (New York: W. W. Norton, 2000).

Recent writing on Bach's music intended for general readers in English are Markus Rathey, *Bach's Major Vocal Works: Music, Drama, Liturgy* (New Haven: Yale University Press, 2016), which includes essays on the *Mass in B Minor* and on the *Christmas Oratorio*; and Daniel R. Melamed, *Hearing Bach's Passions* (New York: Oxford University Press, 2005; updated paperback ed., 2016), which treats problems of listening to Bach's music today.

Mass in B Minor

A score of Bach's *Mass in B Minor* is available in a reprint by Dover Publications of the nineteenth-century Bach-Gesellschaft edition and online at www.imslp.org. The volumes of the *Neue Bach Ausgabe* (NBA, the modern complete edition) related to the *Mass in B Minor* include the edition by Friedrich Smend (II/1); Uwe Wolf's edition (II/1a) of the 1733 Dresden *Missa*, the "Credo in unum Deum," and the 1724 Sanctus (collectively called "Early Versions Pertaining to the *Mass in B Minor*"); and a revised edition of the *Mass*, also edited by Uwe Wolf (*New Bach Edition*, rev. ed., Volume 1). Each NBA volume is accompanied by a critical commentary (Kritischer Bericht) that describes sources and explains editorial decisions. A study score of the work in the text of the NBA is published by Bärenreiter. A different approach is taken in the edition and study score by Joshua Rifkin (Breitkopf & Härtel, 2006), particularly in separating the readings of the 1733 Dresden *Missa* from the complete *Mass*.

Facsimiles are available of Bach's autograph score (Cassel: Bärenreiter) and the 1733 Dresden parts (out of print). These sources are also available on the website Bach Digital (www.bach-digital.de), which provides access to most of the original Bach sources.

There are dozens of recordings of the *Mass in B Minor* in print and available on streaming services. The examples on the companion website to this book are drawn principally from the recording conducted by John Butt (Linn), which uses Rifkin's edition and employs forces of a size and disposition likely to have been heard in Bach's time, including the assignment of one or two singers to each vocal line.

Of the many other recordings available (and there is something for every taste), I return most often to the version conducted by Gustav Leonhardt in 1990 (Deutsche Harmonia Mundi). Among influential earlier recordings is the first conducted by Robert Shaw, in 1947 (RCA Victor). Nikolas Harnoncourt's first recording, in 1968 (Teldec), was a landmark in historical performance practice. Rifkin's recording of 1982 (Nonesuch) was the first to realize the work with minimal forces. The older history of recordings of the *Mass in B Minor* is traced by Teri Noel Towe in Alan Blyth, ed., *Choral Music on Record* (Cambridge: Cambridge University Press, 1991). More recent recordings are listed at www.bach-cantatas.com.

The literature on the *Mass in B Minor* is large. There are surveys by John Butt, *Bach: Mass in B Minor* (Cambridge: Cambridge University Press, 1991), an excellent set of short essays; and by George Stauffer, *Bach, the Mass in B Minor: The Great Catholic Mass* (New Haven: Yale University Press, 2003; reissue of a book from G. Schirmer, 1997), particularly strong on contemporary *Mass* repertory. A variety of recent research on the work is in Yo Tomita, Robin A. Leaver, and Jan Smaczny, eds., *Exploring Bach's B-Minor Mass* (Cambridge: Cambridge University Press, 2013).

Two survey essays are Christoph Wolff, "Past, Present and Future Perspectives on Bach's B-Minor Mass," in the 2013 collection mentioned above; and Hans-Joachim Schulze, "The B Minor Mass—Perpetual Touchstone for Bach Research," in *Bach, Handel, Scarlatti: Tercentenary Essays*, edited by Peter Williams (Cambridge: Cambridge University Press, 1985), 311–320.

Chapter 1. Performing the Mass in B Minor in an Age of Choices

On parody in the study of Bach's music, see the entry for this term in *Oxford Composer Companions: J. S. Bach*.

There is a reconstruction of C. P. E. Bach's 1786 concert that included the Credo of his father's *Mass in B Minor* conducted by Hans-Christoph Rademann available on DVD (Accentus ACC20320).

The status of the 1733 Dresden parts in relation to the 1749 *Mass in B Minor* has been the principal topic of debate among the works' recent editors in the editions cited above.

Friedrich Smend's ideas about the *Mass in B Minor* are reflected in his NBA edition, cited above, and summarized in the English-language preface to the score. The article claiming (unconvincingly) that Bach provided alternative Lutheran and Roman versions is Eduard Van Hengel and Kees Van Houten, "'Et incarnatus': An Afterthought? Against the 'Revisionist' View of Bach's *B-Minor Mass*," *Journal of Musicological Research* 23 (2004): 81–112.

The Notre Dame performance on DVD is directed by John Nelson (Virgin Classics 3706369).

For a scholarly treatment of the problem of buying chocolate, see Stephen Jay Gould, "Phyletic Size Decrease in Hershey Bars," reprinted in Stephen Jay Gould, *Hen's Teeth and Horse's Toes* (New York: W. W. Norton, 1983), 177–186.

Chapter 2. Listening to Parody in the Mass in B Minor

The classic statement of the intentional fallacy as a problem is in W. K. Wimsatt, Jr., and Monroe C. Beardsley, *The Verbal Icon: Studies in the Meaning of Poetry* (Lexington: University of Kentucky Press, 1954).

Ferdinand de Saussure's ideas about synchronic versus diachronic language studies are outlined in his posthumously published *Course in General Linguistics*, available in an English translation by Roy Harris (La Salle, Illinois: Open Court. 1983).

The lost work from which the "Et resurrexit" might be adapted is "Entfernet euch, ihr heitern Sterne" BWV Anh. 9.

Chapter 3. The Musical Topic of the Mass in B Minor

Bernard de Fontenelle's question "Sonata, what do you want of me?" is quoted at the end of the entry "Sonate" in Jean-Jacques Rousseau, *Dictionnaire de musique* (Paris, 1768).

Christmas Oratorio

A score of Bach's *Christmas Oratorio* is available in a reprint by Dover Publications of the nineteenth-century Bach-Gesellschaft edition and online at www.imslp.org. The NBA volume containing the *Christmas Oratorio* is II/6, edited by Walter Blankenburg and Alfred Dürr. A study score of the work in the text of the NBA is published by Bärenreiter. Bach's autograph score of the *Christmas Oratorio* is available in facsimile (Cassel: Bärenreiter, 1984), and both it and the original performing parts are available on Bach Digital (www.bach-digital.de).

The text and a meticulously annotated English translation of the *Christmas Oratorio* are available in Michael Marissen, *Bach's Oratorios: The Parallel German-English Texts, with Annotations* (New York: Oxford University Press, 2008). The original text print is reproduced in Werner Neumann, ed., *Sämtliche von Johann Sebastian Bach vertonte Texte* (Leipzig: Deutscher Verlag für Musik, 1974), and in the critical commentary to the NBA edition.

Recordings of the *Christmas Oratorio* are listed at www.bach-cantatas.com. The examples from the *Christmas Oratorio* on the companion website to this book are drawn from the recording conducted by John Butt (Linn), which uses forces modeled on Bach's. Another recording of the first three parts along these lines is conducted by Holger Eichhorn (Querstand).

There are overviews of the *Christmas Oratorio* in English by Ignace Bossuyt, *Johann Sebastian Bach: Christmas Oratorio (BWV 248)* (Leuven: Leuven University Press, 2004); and in German by Alfred Dürr, *Johann Sebastian Bach, Weihnachts-Oratorium BWV 248* (Munich: W. Fink, 1967); Walter Blankenburg, *Das Weihnachts-Oratorium von Johann Sebastian Bach* (Cassel: Bärenreiter, 1982); and Walter Meinrad, *Johann Sebastian Bach: Weihnachtsoratorium* (Cassel: Bärenreiter, 2006). Markus Rathey's recent study, *Johann Sebastian Bach's Christmas Oratorio: Music, Theology, Culture* (New York: Oxford University Press, 2016), is especially useful for its insights into the work's place in the context of the celebration of Christmas in Germany and into theological matters. The work's role in Bach's oratorio output figures in several essays in Daniel R. Melamed, ed., *J. S. Bach and the Oratorio Tradition*, Bach Perspectives 8 (Urbana: University of Illinois Press, 2011).

Chapter 4. Parody and Its Consequences in the Christmas Oratorio

The early history of the music of parts V and VI, before the church cantata whose parts were reused, is based on unpublished research by Joshua Rifkin and members of a seminar at Boston University.

The best documented of Bach's cantatas for royalty is "Preise dein Glücke, gesegnetes Sachsen" BWV 215. Its themes are subject to an interesting social analysis in David Yearsley, "Princes of War and Peace and Their Most Humble, Most Obedient Court Composer," *Konturen* 1 (2008), http://journals.oregondigital.org/konturen/article/view/1276/1306.

Chapter 5. Listening to the Christmas Oratorio with a Calendar

The liturgical conditions of Bach's work in Leipzig are discussed in Günther Stiller, *Johann Sebastian Bach and Liturgical Life in Leipzig*, edited by Robin A. Leaver, translated by Herbert J. A. Bouman et al. (St. Louis: Concordia, 1984).

Lorenz Mizler's specifications for the length of church cantatas appear in his *Musikalische Bibliothek* (Leipzig, 1754), IV:108–109.

On Bach's congregations, see Tanya Kevorkian, *Baroque Piety: Religion, Society and Music in Leipzig, 1650–1750* (Aldershot: Ashgate, 2007).

Karl Geiringer and Irene Geiringer's biography is *Johann Sebastian Bach: The Culmination of an Era* (New York: Oxford University Press, 1967). Friedrich Blume's *Protestant Church Music: A History* (New York: W.W. Norton, 1974) regarded the second half of the eighteenth century as a period of "Decline and Restoration."

Buxtehude's Lübeck *Abendmusiken* as a model for Bach are discussed in Kerala J. Snyder, "Oratorio on Five Afternoons: From the Lübeck Abendmusiken to Bach's *Christmas Oratorio*," in *Bach and the Oratorio Tradition*, Bach Perspectives 8, edited by Daniel R. Melamed (Urbana: University of Illinois Press, 2011), 69–95.

Multiday Passions are discussed in Daniel R. Melamed, "Multi-Day Passions and J. S. Bach's *Christmas Oratorio*, BWV 248," *Eighteenth-Century Music* 11 (2014): 215–234.

Chapter 6. The Christmas Oratorio in the Shadow of Bach's Passions

The cultural background of Mendelssohn's 1829 performance of the *St. Matthew Passion* with the Berlin Sing-Akademie is explored in Celia Applegate, *Bach in Berlin: Nation and Culture in Mendelssohn's Revival of the St. Matthew Passion* (Ithaca: Cornell University Press, 2005).

The history of the *Christmas Oratorio*'s revival and reception presented here is indebted to Carolyn Carrier-McClimon, "Hearing the 'Töne eines Passionsliedes' in J. S. Bach's *Christmas Oratorio*: The Nineteenth-Century Critical Reception of BWV 248," *Bach: Journal of the Riemenschneider Bach Institute of Baldwin Wallace University* 45, no. 2 (2014): 34–67.

The 1916 article by Gerhard Freiesleben is "Ein neuer Beitrag zur Entstehungsgeschichte von J. S. Bachs Weihnachtsoratorium," *Neue Zeitschrift für Musik* 83, nos. 29–30 (1916): 237–238 and Beilage 1–2, discussed in Daniel R. Melamed, "Bach's *Christmas Oratorio*, BWV 248, and the Jews," *Yale Journal of Music and Religion* 1, no. 1, art. 6 (2015), http://elischolar.library.yale.edu/yjmr/vol1/iss1/6/; the more recent articles that took up Freiesleben's ideas are cited there. The history of Bach's *St. Mark Passion* and attempts to reconstruct it are discussed in Melamed, *Hearing Bach's Passions*.

The characterization of a chorus from the *St. John Passion* quoted here appears in Andreas Loewe, *Johann Sebastian Bach's* St. John Passion *(BWV 245): A Theological Commentary* (Leiden: Brill, 2014).

Index

anti-Judaism, 114, 116–119, 121–122
aria, 33, 35–36, 53
   affective character, 85–86
   bassetto, 81
   cradle, 79
   da capo, 37–38
   echo, 79
   love duet, 27–28, 82–84
   rage, 84–85
   sleep, 78
   trumpet, 79–80
   tutti/choral, 35, 67, 76–77

Bach, Wilhelm Friedemann
   arrangement of J. S. Bach, "Ein feste Burg" BWV 80, 109
Bach, Carl Philipp Emanuel, 4–5, 105, 109
   Heilig H. 778, 5
   Magnificat H. 772, 5
   passion settings, 109
   as supposed author of *Christmas Oratorio*, 110
Bach, Johann Ludwig, 90
Bach, Johann Sebastian
   dating of performances, 93–94
   image, 109–110
   performing ensembles, 90
   revival, 3, 18
   use of music after 1750, 108–109
   working repertory, 6–7, 90, 93–94
Bach, Johann Sebastian (works)
   Ascension Oratorio BWV 11, 95, 105
   "Weinen, Klagen, Sorgen Zagen" BWV 12, 25–26
   "Herr Gott, dich loben wir" BWV 16, 98
   "Wir danken dir, Gott, wir danken dir" BWV 29, 33
   "Freue dich, erlöste Schar" BWV 30, 69, 72, 76
   "Angenehmes Wiederau" BWV 30a, 72
   "Schauet doch und sehet" BWV 46, 29
   "Schauet doch und sehet" BWV 46/1, 38
   "Selig ist der Mann" BWV 57, 38, 89
   "Ich ende behände mein irdisches Leben" BWV 57/7, 38
   "Sehet, welch eine Liebe hat uns der Vater erzeiget" BWV 64, 89
   "Sie werden aus Saba alle kommen" BWV 65, 92

Bach, Johann Sebastian (works) (*Cont.*)
"Jesu, der du meine Seele" BWV 78, 26
"Ein feste Burg ist unser Gott" BWV 80, 109
"Ich habe genung" BWV 82, 78
  "Schlummert ein, ihr matten Augen" BWV 82/3, 78
"Herr Gott, Beherrscher aller Dinge" BWV 120a, 29–30, 34–35
"Durchlauchster Leopold" BWV 173, 73
"Erhöhtes Fleisch und Blut" BWV 173a, 73
"Lass, Fürsten, lass noch einen Strahl" BWV 199, 115
"Schweigt stille, plaudert nicht" BWV 211 [*Coffee Cantata*], 75
"Lasst uns sorgen, lasst uns wachen" BWV 213, 27, 36, 66–67
  "Lasst uns sorgen, lasst uns wachen" BWV 213/1, 69
  "Schlafe, mein Liebster" BWV 213/3, 78–79
  "Treues Echo dieser Orten" BWV 213/5, 79
  "Ich will dich nicht hören" BWV 213/9, 84–86, 123–4
  "Ich bin deine, du bist meine" BWV 213/11, 27, 82
  "Lust der Völker, Lust der Deinen" BWV 213/13, 35–36, 68–69
"Tönet, ihr Pauken! Erschallet, Trompeten" BWV 214, 66–67, 80
  "Tönet, ihr Pauken! Erschallet, Trompeten" BWV 214/1, 32
  "Blast die wohlgegriffnen Flöten" BWV 214/3, 68–70, 80
  "Kron und Preis gekrönter Damen" BWV 214/7, 79
"Preise dein Glücke, gesegnetes Sachsen" BWV 215, 29, 75
"Preise dein Glücke, gesegnetes Sachsen" BWV 215/1, 33
"Durch die von Eifer entflammeten Waffen" BWV 215/7, 80–81
"Jesu, meine Freude" BWV 227, 12
Mass in B Minor BWV 232
  "Kyrie eleison I," 58–60, 62
  "Christe eleison," 53
  "Kyrie eleison II," 14, 48–49, 53, 55, 60
  "Gloria in excelsis Deo," 31, 34, 54
  "Et in terra pax," 31, 54, 57–58
  "Laudamus te," 49–53
  "Gratias agimus tibi," 33, 44, 56–57, 60–62
  "Domine Deus/Domini Fili," 30, 36–39, 53
  "Qui tollis peccata mundi," 29–30, 36, 38, 54
  "Qui sedes ad dextram Patris," 53
  "Quoniam tu solus sanctus," 31, 53
  "Cum Sancto Spiritu," 31, 57–58
  "Credo in unum Deum," 55–58, 60
  "Patrem omnipotentem," 13, 61
  "Et in unum Dominum," 8–11, 26–28, 53, 82–83
  "Et incarnatus est," 8–13, 62
  "Crucifixus," 8–10, 25–26, 28, 62
  "Et resurrexit," 31, 34–36, 54
  "Et iterum venturus est" [in "Et resurrexit"], 35
  "Et in Spiritum Sanctum, 53
  "Confiteor unum baptisma," 13–16, 30, 44–49, 53, 60
  "Et expecto resurrectionem," 13, 15–16, 29–30, 34–35, 54
  "Sanctus," 6–8, 14, 30, 62

"Pleni sunt coeli"
  [in "Sanctus"], 32, 57–58
"Osanna in excelsis," 28–30,
  33, 54
"Benedictus," 30, 53
"Agnus Dei," 53
"Dona nobis pacem," 33, 44,
  56, 61–62
Kyrie-Gloria, 6–8, 22, 31
Credo, 5, 8–14, 22, 47
Berlin Sing-Akademie
  performance, 113
C. P. E. Bach benefit
  performance, 5
Catholic/Lutheran character,
  11–12
"early version," 7
editions, 10–11
instrumental participation,
  13–16
"Mass in B Minor" title, 11,
musical forces, 16–20
musical text, 3–12
musical topic, 40–62
old and new styles, 43–44,
  55–58, 60–61
original score, 4–10, 13–16, 31
parody origin, 21–39, 65
recordings, 10, 15, 19
passages set twice, 13
"Dresden Missa" BWV 232^{I},
  6–8, 14, 43
Masses BWV 233–236, 21–22
Sanctus BWV 238, 33–34
Magnificat BWV 243, 109
  "Et misericordia, 83
St. Matthew Passion BWV 244,
  42, 73, 103–104, 109–113
  "Aus Liebe will mein
    Heiland sterben" BWV
    244/49, 81
  "Kommt, ihr Töchter, helft
    mir klagen" BWV
    244/1, 76
  performance by Berlin
    Sing-Akademie, 18,
    108–109, 124

St. John Passion BWV 245, 12,
  103, 109, 121
  "Herr, unser Herrscher"
    BWV 245/1, 76
  "Jesum von Nazareth" BWV
    245/2b, 121
  "Wir haben keinen König"
    BWV 245/23f, 122
  "Ruht wohl, ihr heiligen
    Gebeine" BWV 245/39, 109
St. Mark Passion BWV 247, 73,
  115, 119–120
  "Geh, Jesu, geh zu deiner
    Pein" BWV 247/1, 76
  "Kreuzige ihn" BWV
    247/33b, 120–122
  "Pfui dich, wie fein zerbrichst
    du den Tempel" BWV
    247/39b, 114–119
Christmas Oratorio BWV 248
  part I, 70, 77, 80, 89, 92–93,
    97–98
  part II, 70, 77, 80, 89, 92–93,
    97–98
  part III, 70, 77, 80, 89, 92–93,
    97–98, 106
  part IV, 69–70, 77, 80, 91–93,
    94–95, 98–99
  part V, 69–73, 77, 91–93, 117
  part VI, 69, 73, 77, 91–93
  "Jauchzet, frohlocket, auf,
    preiset die Tage" BWV
    248/1, 32, 77, 80, 89, 96
  "Bereite dich, Zion" BWV
    248/4, 84–86, 111, 123–4
  "Wie soll ich dich
    empfangen?" BWV 248/5,
    111–113, 124
  "Grosser Herr, o starker
    König" BWV 248/8,
    37, 79
  Sinfonia BWV 248/10,
    77, 96
  "Fürchtet euch nicht"
    BWV 248/13, 80
  "Schlafe, mein Liebster"
    BWV 248/19, 37, 78–79

Bach, Johann Sebastian (works) (*Cont.*)
"Ehre sei Gott in der Höhe" BWV 248/21, 120, 122–124
"Herrscher des Himmels, erhöre das Lallen" BWV 248/24, 77, 96–97
"Lasset uns nun gehen gen Bethlehem" BWV 248/26, 119–120
"Er hat sein Volk getröst" BWV 248/27, 82
"Dies hat er alles uns getan" BWV 248/28, 82
"Herr, dein Mitleid, dein Erbarmen" BWV 248/29, 82
"Schliesse, mein Herze, dies selige Wunder" BWV 248/31, 68–70
"Seid froh dieweil" BWV 248/35, 97
"Fallt mit Danken, fallt mit Loben" BWV 248/36, 77
"Flösst, mein Heiland" BWV 248/39, 79, 99
"Ehre sei dir, Gott, gesungen" BWV 248/43, 68, 77
"Wo ist der neugeborne König der Jüden?" BWV 248/45, 114–119, 122
"Erleucht auch meine finstre Sinnen" BWV 248/47, 73, 81–82
"Herr, wenn die stolzen Feinde schnauben" BWV 248/54, 71–72, 77
"Nur ein Wink von seinen Händen" BWV 248/57, 72
"Was will der Höllen Schrecken nun?" BWV 248/63, 106
"Nun seid ihr wohl gerochen" BWV 248/64, 97, 106, 112–113
autograph score, 65, 69–71, 88, 116, 123–124
concluding movements, 97
as culmination of Christmas oratorio tradition, 99–101
edition, 110
gospel, 95–99
instrumentation, 69, 89, 94–96, 98–99, 106
librettist, 68, 73–74, 86, 97
in liturgy, 89
as multiday oratorio, 99–101, 104–107
opening choruses, 77
as oratorio, 95
original performing parts, 70–71, 88, 94–95
parody origin, 21, 65–87, 110
"passion chorale," 111–113
performance history (Bach), 92–95
performance history (modern), 90–91, 113–114
planning and creation, 68, 70–75, 95–96, 110,
as single work, 88, 92–93, 95, 105–107
reception, 108–124
relation to calendar, 88–107
relation to passions, 108–124
Easter Oratorio BWV 249, 95, 105
"Entfliehet, verschwindet, entweichet, ihr Sorgen" BWV 249a, 95
Well-Tempered Clavier BWV 846–893, 110
Capriccio on the Departure of a Most Beloved Brother BWV 992, 41
Concerto for two violins BWV 1043, 59
Canon "Christus Coronabit Crucigeros" BWV 1077, 9
"Credo in unum Deum" BWV 1081, 55
"Entfernet euch, ihr heitern Sterne" BWV Anh. 9, 35
"Es lebe der König, der Vater im Lande" BWV Anh. 11, 29, 33

Mass [attrib] BWV Anh. 167, 109
cantatas for Christmas, 88–89
cantatas for Sunday after
 Christmas, 93
cantatas for New Year's, 91
cantatas for Sunday after
 New Year's, 92
cantatas for Epiphany, 91–92
cantatas for Lent, 104–105
lost church cantata model
 for *Christmas Oratorio*
 part VI BWV 248/Va,
 70–71
lost secular cantata model for
 Christmas Oratorio parts
 V-VI BWV deest, 71–72
passions, 4, 19
Bassani, Giovanni Battista,
 Missa V from *Acroama missale*,
 55–56
Beethoven, Ludwig van, 109, 24
 Symphony No. 9, 23–24
Berlin Sing-Akademie, 18,
 108–109, 113
Brockes, Barthold Heinrich, 103
Bugenhagen, Johann, 102
Buxtehude, Dieterich
 Abendmusiken, 101, 104

cantata
 construction, 76
 dated texts, 109
 length, 89
 sacred and secular, 75–76
chocolate, 3–4, 18, 20
Christmas season
 celebration, 91
 Epiphany, 91–92, 97, 99
 gospel readings, 95–96
 invented oratorio tradition,
  100–101
 motets, 122–124
 New Year's Day, 23, 75, 91–94, 98
 Sunday after Christmas, 92–93
 Sunday after New Year's, 92
counterpoint. *See* style (old)
"crowd chorus," 121–122

Doles, Johann Friedrich, 109
dramma per musica, 27, 35, 66–67, 72,
 75, 78–80, 106
Dresden
 electoral court, 6, 27, 29, 43–44,
  66, 74-75. 80, 115
 homage works, 29, 66, 74–75, 81

Fama (Pheme), 79–80
Feast of the Circumcision
 (New Year's Day), 91, 98
Fiddler on the Roof, xvii
flute
 military associations, 80–82
 pastoral associations, 96
Fontanelle, Bernard, de 41
Freiesleben, Gerhard, 114–121

"Gelobet seist du, Jesu Christ," 111
genetic fallacy, 24–25, 84
Gottsched, Johann Christoph, xv-xvii
Graupner, Christoph, 101

Handel, George Frideric, xviii
 Brockes Passion, 103
 Giulio Cesare in Egitto, 85
 Messiah, 5, 85, 96, 113
 Semele, 78
harmonized gospel, 102
Harrer, Gottlob, 109
Haydn, Franz Joseph, 41, 109
Henrici, Christian Friedrich
 (Picander), 73–4
"Herzlich tut mich verlangen," 112
horn
 characteristic key, 98–99
 hunt associations, 41
 as marker of festivity, 69, 89,
  91–92, 98–99
Hunold, Christian Friedrich
 (Menantes), xv-xviii

intentional fallacy, 23–24, 83–84

Jackson, Michael, xvii
"Jesaia dem Propheten das
 geschah," 113

Keiser, Reinhard
   Brockes Passion, 103–104
Kelly, Grace, 42

lament 26, 28
Leipzig
   churches, 89–91
   Collegium Musicum, 66, 75
   hymns, 112–113
   observance of Christmas, 88–92
   St. Nicholas Church, 6, 89–92
   St. Thomas Church, 6, 89–92
   St. Thomas School, 6–7, 75, 94, 99, 118
   tempus clausum, 104–105
   Thomascantors, 99–100, 109
   town council inauguration, 33
   University, 75, 90, 118
   Zimmerman's Coffee House, 66, 75
linguistics, 24
liturgical calendar, 88–99, 102–104
Lully, Jean-Baptiste
   Atys, 78
Luther, Martin, 118
   "Jesaia, dem Propheten, das geschah," 30

Mad magazine, xvii
Matheson, Johann,
   Brockes Passion, 103
Mendelssohn, Felix, 18, 108, 113
   Christus, 116–117
Mizler, Lorenz, 89
Monteverdi Claudio
   Lamento della ninfa, 26
musical meaning, 23–25, 40–42
musical topics
   hunt, 41
   march, 41
   pastoral, 77, 96

Neumeister, Erdmann, 76
Nicene Creed, 9, 26, 55

"O Haupt voll Blut und Wunden," 111–112
old and new styles in church music, 43
oratorio—textual construction, 67, 95–97, 119

Palestrina, Giovanni Pierluigi da, 14, 43, 48, 58, 122
   Missa Ecce sacerdos magnus, 48
   Missa sine nomine, 48
parody, xv–xviii, 21–39, 65–87
   audibility, 22, 25, 28, 33–34, 65–66, 86–87
   definition, xv, xvii, 68
   as mode of invention, xvi
   study, 21–22, 25, 65, 86
   types, 21–22
"passion Chorale," 111–114
passions
   multiday, 101–104
   as oratorios, 67, 95
   poetic, 103
poetry
   cat, xv–xviii
   parodied, xv–xvii
   set to music, 32–35
Offspring, The, xvii
performance (eighteenth century)
   Bach's ensembles, 90
   singers and instrumentalists, 17–18
   vocal forces, 16–18
performance (modern), 3–20, 35, 86, 88
   1950s, and 1960s, 16–17
   1970s historical performance movement, 16amateur vs. professional, 19–20
   "crowd choruses," 121–122
   nineteenth century, 18, 108–109, 113–114, 118–119, 124
   vocal forces, 18–19
Purcell, Henry
   Dido and Aeneas, 26

reconstruction of lost works, 85, 114–119
Rietz, Julius, 15
Rilling, Helmuth, 15
ritornello. *See* style (modern)
Rousseau, Jean-Jacques, 41
Rust, Wilhelm, 110

Sanctus settings, 32
Saussure, Ferdinand de, 24
Schelle, Johann
  Actus musicus for Christmas, 99–100
Schiller, Friedrich, 23
Schumann, Robert, 113
Schütz, Heinrich
  Christmas Historia, 79, 100
scores and performing parts, 7, 14, 71, 73
sculpture, Greek and Roman, 16
Smend, Friedrich, 11–13, 15
sommeil, 78
Stölzel, Gottfried Heinrich, 90, 101
style (modern), 49–53
  affective character, 25, 41, 46–47, 75–76, 84–86
  choral phrase structure, 32–35
  choral ritornello movements, 28–30, 53–55
  extended, 57–60
  immediate vocal openings, 30–31, 38, 54
  instrumental writing, 49–50
  ritornello form, 50–53
  ritornello phrase structure, 51
style (old), 44–49
  affect neutrality, 15, 47, 61
  basso continuo, 47, 49, 55
  cantus firmus, 46
  counterpoint, 14, 45, 50
  extended, 55–57

notation, 47–48
phrase structure, 50–51
voices and instruments, 13–16, 44
style
  eggs, 42
  musical, 42–43
symmetry, 12

Tate, Nahum
  Dido and Aeneas, 26
Telemann, Georg Philipp, 42, 103, 105
  Brockes Passion, 103
tempus clausum, 104–105
theological interpretation, speculative, 9, 12, 81–83, 111–112, 120
topics. *See* musical topics
trumpet
  association with Fama, 79–80
  characteristic key, 69, 96–99, 106
  as marker of festivity, 30–31, 47, 75, 88–89, 91–92, 96–99, 104, 108, 112
  in old style, 56–57, 60–62
  royal associations, 57, 79–80

Victoria, Tomás Luis de
  "O quam gloriosum," 21
  Missa O quam gloriosum, 21
Vivaldi, Antonio, 42
"Vom Himmel hoch, da komm ich her," 80, 111

Wagner, Richard, 117
  Parsifal, 118
Winterfeld. Carl, von, 111–112
"Wir Christenleut," 97
Wolzogen, Hans von, 118

Yankovic, Weird Al, xvii

Zelter, Carl Friedrich, 18

www.ingramcontent.com/pod-product-compliance
Ingram Content Group UK Ltd.
Pitfield, Milton Keynes, MK11 3LW, UK
UKHW041302180426
11947UKWH00009B/627